Praise for
A Path Beyond Post-Traumatic Stress

"I started reading the manuscript for this book because Anna Goodwin asked me to see how she was utilizing my poem "The Healing Wall" throughout the book. She also asked me to share my honest response as a veteran to what she was saying. It took less than three pages for me to realize I wasn't reading a book about someone else with PTS, I was reading about me! That realization caught me off guard. And in so many unexpected ways, this book has changed my life. I know it will do the same for you."

—Patrick Overton, Ph.D. in communications, and Vietnam veteran
Author of *Rebuilding the Front Porch of America: Essays on the Art of Community Making*

"Anna Goodwin has written an extremely important book for friends and families, and most of all for anyone who has been affected by a crisis or trauma. She artfully describes the challenge of responding to trauma in the most effective and accessible way to achieve health and wholeness. I am excited to use Anna's book in my psychotherapy practice working with healing emotional wounds."

—Neil Bricco, M.S., LCPC, Psychotherapist
Author of *Wisdom of the Wound: Discovering a Path to Wholeness*

"I have found in my personal and professional experience, many people have PTS and PTSD symptoms. These symptoms are often misunderstood or undetected and often go untreated for lack of understanding on the part of family, friends as well as denial on the part of the individual. PTSD symptoms impact a person's behavior and interaction with others, as well as their ability to function on a daily basis. Anna has written an excellent book that is very helpful for individuals suffering from stress after a trauma as well as families, friends, and professionals to assist in understanding and treating PTSD.

> —Kathy Crawford, LCSW, Psychotherapist in private practice

This beautifully written book is a must for those who have a spouse or loved one who has suffered trauma, whether at the hand of someone else, a natural disaster, or the invisible wounds of war. I am an incest survivor – thriver, and author of *The Fifth Sister*. We five sisters survived sustained childhood trauma. Each of us carried into adulthood responses to that upbringing. I have PTS. I can say from personal experience that Ms. Goodwin's book is spot on – for those who have experienced trauma and for those who love them. She guides and supports those who have suffered, and informs and assists their spouses and children. She offers hope. Wading through the emotional labyrinth brought on by trauma can be confusing. . . tricky even. This book is simply written and will make it easier for you to recover.

> —Laura Landgraf, incest survivor and author of *The Fifth Sister*

"Anna Goodwin has written an easily read, helpful and thoroughly authoritative guide. It should be read by all those who've experienced battle or other trauma and by all who come in contact with them."
 —Jim Minard, Sleep Researcher

Non-Fiction Books

Also by E. Anna Goodwin

Sandplay Therapy: A Step-by-Step Manual for Psychotherapists of Diverse Orientations
Barbara L. Boik and E. Anna Goodwin
published by W.W. Norton (2000)

How to Cope with Stress after Trauma: Especially for Veterans, their Families, and Friends
E. Anna Goodwin,
published by Bitterroot Mountain Publishing (2014)

A PATH BEYOND
POST-TRAUMATIC STRESS:
STEPS TO RECOVERY AND RESILIENCE

What you need to know to help yourself
or someone you love.

E. ANNA GOODWIN, M.S., NCC

Bitterroot Mountain Publishing
Hayden, Idaho

A Path Beyond Post Traumatic Stress:
Steps to Resilience and Recovery

© 2019 by E. Anna Goodwin

All names and identifying characteristics of clients described in this book have been changed.

Published by Bitterroot Mountain Publishing House LLC
4319 Echo Glenn Lane, Coeur d'Alene, ID 83815
BMPHmedia.com

Interior design by Jera Publishing
Cover design by Deb Schmit

Authors website: www.anaparkergoodwin.com

All rights reserved. This book or parts thereof, may not be reproduced in any form without permission, except by a reviewer who may quote brief passages in a review to be printed in magazines, newspapers, or on the web.

The ideas, procedures, and suggestions in this book are intended to supplement, not replace, the medical and psychological advice of trained professionals. The author and publisher disclaim any liability arising directly or indirectly from the use of this book.

For permission to reproduce excerpts of this publication please contact:
Bitterroot Mountain Publishing House at info@BMPHmedia.com

Library of Congress Control Number: 2018908971
ISBN: 978-1-940025-40-7

Printed in the United States of America

1. Post Trauma Stress—Recovery 2. Cope with stress—After trauma
3. Anxiety and depression—After stress 4. Trauma survivors and Families—PTS Recovery I. Title.

Contents

Introduction 1
Whom is this book for? 4
How to Use This Book 8
Post-Trauma Stress Test 11

PART 1: The facts about stress after a trauma 15
What Are PTS and PTSD? 16
A definition of Post Trauma Stress and Post Traumatic
    Stress Disorder 21
Where does the diagnosis of PTSD originate? 25
What types of trauma can cause PTS or PTSD? 26
How often does PTSD occur? 29
What qualifies as an unusual and/or severe trauma? 30
Are some people more vulnerable to PTS and PTSD
    than others? 33
What are the symptoms of PTS and PTSD? 38
What happens in the brain and body during PTS? 49

PART 2: Twenty Steps to Help You Heal 57
It's time to deal with your trauma. 59
Characteristics of a Resilient Person 60
What makes people happy? 62
Step One: Become stable. 63
Step Two: Stay connected to other people and animals. 75

Step Three: Empower yourself. 84

Step Four: Learn to relax. 97

Step Five: Become aware of yourself. 103

Step Six: Check with a doctor to see whether medications can help. 112

Step Seven: Change your thinking.. 117

Step Eight: Change unwanted behaviors 134

Step Nine: Work with your emotions ("energy in motion"). . . 140

Step Ten: Reconnect spiritually. 160

Step Eleven: Deal with memories. 171

Step Twelve: Take responsibility for yourself. You have choices. . 188

Step Thirteen: Deal with alcohol and drug addictions.. 194

Step Fourteen: Use your creativity. 199

Step Fifteen: Have fun. Learn to play again. Enjoy yourself and laugh. 206

Step Sixteen: Spend time in nature. 209

Step Seventeen: Work with your physical body. 212

Step Eighteen: Rebuild your purpose in life. Volunteer your time or look into getting a meaningful job. 226

Step Nineteen: Explore new technologies. 232

Step Twenty: Try these special techniques.. 237

Conclusion 243

PART 3: Families and Friends. 245

Introduction to Families and Friends 247

What you can do to help the person you love.. 249

What you need to do to take care of yourself. 264

What your children need. 272

The Healing Wall (The complete poem) 277
Suggested Readings. 284
Acknowledgements 287
About the Author 289

Introduction

Why did I write a book to help survivors and their families deal with the trauma they have faced in their lives? As a former psychotherapist, an important part of my many years of work specializing in Post Traumatic Stress Disorder (PTSD), has been building an understanding of the unique issues people with Post Trauma Stress (PTS) face. But more importantly I learned how to help my clients recover, become resilient, and flourish.

On a more personal level, I knew a man who was severely traumatized by what happened to him as an adolescent. I'd like to tell you about the traumas he faced, but I can't. Why? Because he rarely spoke of them. He never admitted, maybe not even to himself, that something had happened that changed him forever. He did his best to hide his emotions, but regardless of how hard he tried to repress his experiences, his wife and two children could tell when the memories flashed. Sometimes he screamed out in the night and walked the floor. After those nights he became withdrawn, anxious, and depressed. He wouldn't speak to anyone for days. Then he would burst into uncontrollable rages for what seemed no reason. There were times his family worried he would hurt someone or himself.

This man lived with the trauma of war most of his life. Was he a veteran? No. He was a refugee. Every day from age 12 to age 18, he faced the terror of war, starvation, and death.

He and his family spent 6 years running and hiding, fighting for their lives during the Russian Revolution and the early Stalin purges. How do I know that the story is true? He was my father, and I was his youngest daughter. Often I felt torn inside, wondering if I was somehow to blame for his struggles. I wished I could help, but I didn't know what to do.

As my father suffered day after day, so did my mother, my sister, and I. And after a while I became very angry at him. Why? Because I did not understand what was going on and I couldn't fix him regardless how hard I tried to do everything "right." And it was not until I became a psychotherapist and learned about Post Traumatic Stress that I finally "got it" and could feel deep compassion for him and forgive him.

My father passed away several years ago. Did it matter that he rarely talked about what had happened to him? I don't know. He was an ardent rancher who loved the earth. He spent most of his time working alone on acres of land. I knew him as a good and honest Christian man, but a somber man who rarely mingled in large groups. However according to his sisters, before the war he had been a talkative, outgoing youth who loved to laugh and have fun.

What troubled me the most was that he never received the help he needed. Thus he never recovered. And I never learned to know the real person—the happy, compassionate, and loving father—of whom I only caught glimpses.

Although your circumstances and your trauma will have been different than my father's, the symptoms and results may well be similar. If you have been traumatized you will need to deal with the consequences. I hope this book will help you and your family recover and become more resilient.

Introduction

The reason I chose psychotherapy as my profession may well have been related to my father's history. In 1980 I graduated from the University of Maryland with a Master of Science degree in psychological counseling. I later became licensed and nationally certified. I have taught at two universities, conducted numerous workshops nationally on several topics, and spoken on post traumatic stress to both lay and professional groups.

I worked for a crisis counseling center and later ran a large private practice for many years, specializing in counseling children, adults, and families who struggled with Post Traumatic Stress Disorder (PTSD). My clients included survivors of physical and sexual abuse, rape, war, robberies, and shootings, traumatic accidents, and natural disasters as well as first responders and veterans. Five days a week, I listened to seven or eight people per day who had experienced severe traumas. Underneath those often brave exteriors, I recognized the same types of pain for *all* people with Post Traumatic Stress. Together, my clients and I worked to discover techniques that could help them recover. I give them a great deal of credit for many of the ideas shared in this book.

Whom is this book for?

If you, a family member, or significant other has experienced a trauma sometime in your life and you are dealing with the consequences, this book is for you. The event may have been as a child, a teenager, or adult. It may have come from a natural disaster such as flooding or fire, an accident, some kind of abuse, attack, a war, or witnessing and dealing with survivors at a tragic scene (e.g., such as police, firemen, ambulance workers, first responders). The book is also for psychotherapists, counselors, or anyone working with people or family members who have been traumatized. The steps in Section 2 and the steps for family members and children in Section 3 can be used either with individuals, in families, or groups in sessions, or as homework assignments.

If you have picked up *A Path beyond Post Traumatic Stress: Steps to Recovery and Resilience*, you may be concerned there is something "wrong" with you or someone you love. You or they may be experiencing nightmares, sleeplessness, anxiety and anger, and/or depression. Your heart may race and your muscles tense. You may have turned to addictive medications, illegal drugs, or alcohol for relief. You may become overly watchful, your body may shake, or you may jump at unexpected noises or movements. You may avoid anything that triggers memories of traumatic events. Some people relive the trauma they experienced. If you or your loved one has some of these symptoms, please continue reading.

Whom is this book for?

Today, with the fear and constant threat of terrorism and violence on this planet, more and more people are feeling the continual stress of living in what we perceive as a dangerous world. They are always alert, afraid, tense, fearing some kind of life threatening attack that may kill or maim them or their loved ones. Some carry guns to protect themselves and their children.

Remember, perception is often more important than what may be the reality after you look back on it. So what someone else defines as scary but not dangerous, may be much more traumatic to you at the time, depending on how you perceive the situation and your past experiences. Don't deny your feelings or belittle them.

The way I define Post Traumatic Stress (PTS) is that it's a milder condition than full-blown Post Traumatic Stress Disorder (PTSD) with fewer stress symptoms and may have been triggered by less terrifying events. Usually the events make you feel helpless, horrified, and as if you or a loved one might die. I will refer to PTSD as well as PTS, because much more scientific research has been conducted on PTSD. The other reason I refer frequently to PTSD is that the lesser stress symptoms of PTS may lead to a full-blown disorder if neglected for too long.

The strategies and steps offered here are intended for people who have experienced trauma but are still functional, and have not been diagnosed with PTSD. If you have been diagnosed with a "disorder," please seek counseling and medical help first and then add these steps to your recovery strategies where appropriate, and with your counselor's advisement.

If you have what psychologists diagnose as Post Traumatic Stress Disorder (PTSD) you may no longer be capable of leading what most of us would call "normal daily life." Your brain has malfunctioned due to excessive stress. Many people do not wish to acknowledge their problems out of fear of negative repercussions, such as losing their jobs or being stigmatized as weak and "mentally ill."

At this point, let me debunk an old belief that has been alleged for far too many years: people who experience a lot of stress following a trauma are weak. NOT TRUE. The brain is an organ, just like any other organ in the body. The freeze, fight, or flight response is normal. It helps us survive in dangerous situations. But when it continues way past the time the danger is gone it means that the brain is malfunctioning. We don't consider people weak because they have had heart attacks, or because their lungs or kidneys have failed. Neither should we think of people as weak because their brains are not functioning normally.

PTS affects many more people than does PTSD. Survivors with PTS remain functional, at least to some degree, and often have difficulty admitting that they somehow feel "different" than they did before the trauma. Friends and families usually notice these changes before the effected people do or are willing to admit something is wrong, as in the case of Amber.

Since being attacked on a street in Baltimore, Amber, an adolescent began skipping school and isolating, stating she had severe headaches and felt tired and sick to her stomach much of the time. She slept only a couple of hours a night. Her mother noticed she was easily agitated and depressed much of the time but Amber stated she was sure she was just coming down with the flu and her problems had nothing to do with the attack. Finally both her family and friends confronted her and pushed her to seek help. When she saw her school counselor she admitted that she was having nightmares and she was afraid to go outside. When the counselor asked her why she had waited so long to seek help she said she was scared her friends would tease her and leave her if they knew what was really going on.

Like Amber and her family and friends, many people may be grappling with similar issues with little or no help.

How to Use This Book

The strategies in this book work. Many of my clients over the years have used them with great success. Although the verdict is still out on some of the newer technologies, I believe they are worth mentioning so you can explore them if you wish. But regardless of which steps you decide to use, they all require an earnest and dedicated commitment to the healing process.

A Path beyond Post Traumatic Stress: Steps to Resilience and Recovery begins with a self-test to let you determine for yourself your current level of stress. Next I give you some basic information about Post Trauma Stress (PTS) and Post Traumatic Stress Disorder (PTSD). In Part 2 you will find 20 proven and effective steps to stabilize and to deal with your pain, depression, and anxiety. The steps work somewhat like steps on a ladder. As you climb them one by one, they lead you closer and closer to your goal of recovery. In Part 3, I offer family members ways of coping and helping their loved one who has suffered a trauma, as well as themselves and their children.

These steps and strategies form a comprehensive and detailed recovery program for everyone suffering from stress-related issues. I realize that you may feel overwhelmed when you look at all of them at once. Start by choosing only those steps that apply to you and fit with your lifestyle and

How to Use This Book

beliefs. It may take a long time for you to complete a single step. That's okay. Sometimes slower is better.

If you feel unstable at this point, please start with Step One, which focuses on becoming stable. Then choose another step that you are willing to try, and so on. Some steps will work for you and some won't. Don't give up. Choose the ones that help you and practice them. There is a simple difference between those individuals who recover and those who don't: people who recover learn new ways to cope and dedicate their lives to using them.

As brain research surges forward our understanding of PTS is growing rapidly. The information I provide is current as of 2017. We live in an age of groundbreaking brain and memory research, and what is considered factual today may be superseded later by new information. I recommend you check online occasionally for the very latest data.

I wish I could grant you a quick solution to your problems, but at this point I can't. You will never be exactly the same as you were before you underwent a trauma. This is true of all human beings. Each memorable experience changes us. But it's also true that if you are willing to heal from the trauma, you may well change for the better. I have seen positive changes in attitude, inner peace, wisdom, and compassion develop in ways I would never have thought possible. Many of my former clients have gone on to help others with similar experiences and have changed individual lives and the greater world around them.

I have often wished that my clients and their families had understood how to deal with the traumas shortly after they happened. With proper treatment, perhaps their symptoms might have disappeared, or at least not worsened into "disorders."

You deserve to heal and prosper regardless of what you have experienced. If you feel a full recovery is too hard to commit to for yourself at this time, please do it for your loved ones. Even if you're not prepared to do all the steps involved in recovery, read this book anyway, and reread it when you are ready to make positive changes in your life.

Although I mention client's stories, I do not highlight traumatic details experienced. Instead I emphasize recovery after the trauma has occurred. All names of people in the book have been altered and stories are changed somewhat to assure the anonymity of people I know as well as my former clients.

Before you continue, please take this test
to determine your present stress level.

Although there is a widely used assessment tool for PTSD called the Clinical Administrated PTSD Scale or CAPS, it is designed as a structured interview to be used by trained professionals. *The following is not a formal test and has not been researched for validity or reliability.* It is merely a short test I have created using the symptoms described in *The Diagnostic and Statistical Manual of Mental Health Disorders* (*DSM*) to help you compare your levels of stress before the trauma and after. Please answer as honestly as you can. You may choose to share the results with someone else, or keep them private.

Post-Trauma Stress Test

Place a number 1 to 5 in the blank next to each question according to how much you feel the statement applies to you:

Number 1 is "not at all"
Number 2 is "not often or not severe"
Number 3 is "sometimes or moderate"
Number 4 is "often or severe"
Number 5 is "very often or very severe"

1. How frequently do you have recurring dreams or memories of the trauma?

2. How distressing are these memories?

3. How vividly do you remember the trauma in your memories and dreams?

4. How often do you have flashbacks where you feel you are reliving the trauma?

5. How often do you feel like crying when you remember or speak about the trauma?

6. How often do you find yourself avoiding situations that trigger your memories of the trauma?

7. How severely do you think the trauma has affected you?

8. How often have your traumatic experiences or symptoms been ignored or belittled by others?

9. If you experienced trauma as a child, such as abuse, an accident, etc., how severe was it? How often did it occur?

In this portion of the self-test, "Now" means "Today." "Before" means "Before experiencing the traumatic event."

10. How often do you feel distant from other people, even your family? Now ___ Before___

Post-Trauma Stress Test

11. How often do you have problems falling or staying asleep? Now ___ Before ___

12. How easily are you startled when something unexpected occurs? Now ___ Before ___

13. How often do you feel you are unable to function normally? Now ___ Before ___

14. How often are you on the lookout for threats or danger? Now ___ Before ___

15. How angry do you feel? Now ___ Before ___

16. How often do you have difficulty concentrating or feel confused? Now ___ Before ___

17. How often do you feel numb or have no feelings? Now ___ Before ___

18. How often do you experience outbursts of anger? Now ___ Before ___

19. How often are you depressed, anxious, or uninterested in things you used to enjoy? Now ___ Before ___

20. How often do you have symptoms such as a rapid heartbeat, shaking, perspiring, or tense muscles? Now ___ Before ___

21. How often do you think you may not live to be old?
    Now ___ Before ___

22. How often do you think about suicide? Now ___ Before ___

23. If you think about suicide, how detailed are your plans?
    Now ___ Before ___

24. How often do you isolate yourself or spend time alone?
    Now ___ Before ___

25. How often are you ill or in pain? Now ___ Before ___

26. How often do you use alcohol or other drugs (legal or illegal) to help you cope with life? Now ___ Before ___

If most of your answers are marked 3 or under, you are probably a good candidate for the steps in this book. If your answers are mostly over 3, please seek professional help as soon as possible, and use this book in conjunction with more comprehensive therapy.

PART 1

The facts about stress after a trauma, commonly called Post Trauma Stress (PTS) and Post Traumatic Stress Disorder (PTSD)

Accurate information is essential to healing.

Note: You can read this section now, or turn immediately to the steps you need, then return to this information later.

What Are PTS and PTSD?

Years ago, as a psychotherapist working in private practice, I earned a reputation in my community for my work with people who dealt with severe trauma. Social service agencies often referred clients to me, sometimes from as far as two hundred miles away.

A tall, muscular man I'll call Jack, then in his mid-forties, came to me with a severe anxiety disorder. He had worked for his local fire department for more than ten years. About seven years earlier, Jack had resigned because of what he said was "burnout." Since then he had been "fine" although he reluctantly admitted to having problems sleeping and nightmares about a couple of fires and explosions where several people had been killed.

Jack had been employed at a racetrack servicing cars for several years, and he loved his work. About six months ago, however, one of the drivers had run into a wall and his car had caught on fire and had exploded. Soon after, Jack developed a phobia to what he called "loud noise." Every time he heard a car backfire, he jumped, covered his head, and crouched behind something or threw himself on the ground. His heart raced, and he shook for several minutes. Understandably, he decided to change jobs.

What Are PTS and PTSD?

To get the job he wanted he decided to move and attend a university in another area of the country. He expected his phobia to end, but instead, whenever a car backfired or he heard a loud bang, he reacted in a similar way as he had to the racecar. Over the previous couple of months he had spent much of his time trying to avoid loud noises. He had frequent nightmares and woke up sweating. Whenever he felt he had no control over his wife and adolescent children, he exploded at them. His wife was threatening to take the children and leave if the problem didn't stop. In plain words, his life had become unmanageable.

When Jack arrived in my office, I noticed his face was drawn and his hands trembled.

As I always did, I asked him to tell me his family history, starting with his childhood. He told me that his parents were divorced and he had lived with an alcoholic and abusive father. Within less than five minutes, however, he switched from stories about his childhood to stories about his experiences as a fireman. His memories were so vivid, it was as though they had happened yesterday.

In time, Jack dealt with his symptoms, and eventually with his memories. During our year together, Jack did not forget his time as a fireman, running into burning buildings with overhead beams crashing in front of him, explosions all around him, his friends being injured and rushed to the hospital, the people and animals he had not been able to save. Most of all, he never forgot the guilt he felt that often he had been so afraid that he thought he might not have done his best. Yes, the memories were still there, but they were much less intense. They no longer triggered anxiety and nightmares. Jack's anger subsided, and after a time of separation, Jack, his wife, and two children began family therapy.

Why did I start the book with Jack's story? Because of the lessons we can all learn from what he experienced.

THE FIRST LESSON:
Don't make excuses or ignore your first symptoms of post trauma stress. The sooner you deal with the symptoms, the more likely they will recede into the past without you becoming dysfunctional or developing what psychologists call a "disorder."

THE SECOND LESSON:
Although most post trauma stress occurs in the immediate aftermath of a trauma, delayed reactions are common. Months or years may pass before they manifest in the conscious mind. Usually there is a trigger event that sets off the symptoms. For Jack, this event was the explosion of the racecar.

THE THIRD LESSON:
You are strong, not weak, when you face life and deal with it as it happens instead of pretending there's nothing wrong. It is a sign of strength to ask for help. Anyone—and I mean anyone—may have a reaction to trauma similar to Jack's. I hope that some of the steps in this book will help you learn how to cope, but if they don't relieve your symptoms, see a psychotherapist and/or a medical doctor.

THE FOURTH LESSON:
You are not alone, even though you may feel like you are. Certainly each event is unique, to some extent, regarding the specifics of the trauma. It is very important for you to meet with other people who have experienced similar traumas and who can understand you in a way others can't. But regardless of who people are or the type of severe trauma they have been exposed to—whether it occurred in an accident, in a natural disaster, in war, or in an abusive situation— all are human beings. As humans, our bodies and brains control our emotions and minds and tend to respond to trauma in similar ways. Some react more severely, some less so, for a longer or shorter time, but millions around the globe experience similar symptoms. Only the specific circumstances of an individual's trauma vary, not the range of PTS symptoms.

THE FIFTH LESSON:
Recovery is possible. If you get help, your symptoms will most likely disappear or at least lessen to the point where they can be easily managed. Often you become wiser and more compassionate in the process.

Although PTS and PTSD are much more complex than can be addressed here, I hope that this book will give you a basic understanding of what is happening in your body, mind, and emotions. I have deliberately attempted to avoid discussing anything that might trigger your traumatic memories, but if at any time you feel overwhelmed or flooded by emotions as you read, make sure that you stop reading, take some deep breaths, and do something that you love to do and that helps you relax. For many people, physical exercise of any kind helps. Even those people who have been injured can usually work out in some way to exercise. In addition, or if physical exercise doesn't seem to help, read Step One on stabilizing and follow its recommendations.

Information is power and gives you back some of the control you felt you lost during and after the trauma. Most people don't know much about PTS or PTSD, but the sooner you know the facts, the sooner recovery will begin.

Research suggests that there are **three factors that consistently lead to stress: uncertainty, lack of information, and loss of control.** As you learn, you'll find your stress reactions reducing. So when you feel ready, continue reading Part 1 and any other information that you trust. Personal accounts of recovery from others can be very helpful, especially if you identify with them, but make sure you remember that everyone is different and reacts somewhat differently. What worked for one person may not help you, just as some of the steps I provide may not work for you. Try them and find the best ones. Then practice them daily. If you read articles that make exaggerated claims of instant, complete recovery, be careful of the writer's information and suggested techniques. Although I imagine instant recoveries do occur, they are rare. At this stage in time, for most people, recovery is a process that takes time—weeks, months, and sometimes years. But by then the symptoms have receded to such an extent that life is manageable again.

A Definition of Post Trauma Stress and Post Traumatic Stress Disorder

Stress after a trauma is a **normal bodily response** to an unusual and often severe traumatic experience. Often the trauma is perceived as life-threatening to you or the people you love. Symptoms occur most frequently after an event that happens suddenly, repeatedly, or over a long period of time, such as in childhood abuse, domestic violence or war. (Chronic repeated or long lasting traumatic events such as physical, sexual, or emotional abuse are often called Complex PTSD.) The trauma triggers the body's survival mechanism, called the "freeze, fight, or flight" response. A normal reaction to a severe stressor usually includes shock, intense fear, anxiety, numbness, and depression.

The body has an amazing ability to keep you functioning during a crisis, but in the aftermath of the trauma, when the adrenaline and stress hormones stop flowing, some people may collapse or become non-functional. Others have symptoms of trauma but may continue to function. Still others may not experience symptoms until years after the triggering trauma.

Simply stated, Post-Trauma Stress (PTS) is Post Traumatic Stress Disorder (PTSD) without the "disorder." Where do we draw the line between the two? As with most things in life, you will find considerable controversy on the topic, particularly in the military, as more and more armed services personnel are reporting serious symptoms while overseas, and even more so after discharge.

Some neuroscientists now believe Post Trauma Stress is triggered by trauma but is a problem of memory. Those with the best memories suffer the most often and the longest from trauma. With PTS, although bad memories and physical symptoms interfere with a person's everyday life, he or she remains functional enough to continue working and, at least to some degree, to fulfill his or her role as a spouse, parent, friend, employee, family, and community member. Usually severe physical and emotional symptoms last for less than a month after a major stressful event, and the body and emotions automatically normalize to a point the person can once again function. However, they may spend a great deal of energy doing so.

PTSD is a more severe condition than PTS. With PTSD, recovery does not take place so easily. PTSD sufferers' symptoms are so prolonged and severe that they can no longer keep a job, continue normal relationships with family and friends, or function in society on a day-to-day basis. PTS symptoms, if not addressed promptly following a trauma, may develop into PTSD. On the other hand, immediate treatment of PTS symptoms, like most preventative programs, might well save them from the torture and heartache of PTSD.

The following two case studies illustrate the far-reaching effects of PTS. See if you recognize yourself or a loved one in either of these stories.

A Definition of PTS and PTSD

Janet and Maureen both lived through the Yellowstone fires. Both lost their family homes and all their belongings. Both lost a close friend in the fire. After the fire Janet broke up with her boyfriend and decided to become a nurse. However, she was only able to work for a few years before her PTS-induced memories and reactions became so severe that she could no longer function. Except for sleep medication and anxiety-reducing drugs she refused treatment, too proud to admit she needed help. Meanwhile, her symptoms continued to escalate. When she went to the woods or even drove through parts of the forest she had panic attacks. Eventually she went out less and less and began to isolate. She became more and more depressed and added alcohol and other drugs to the mix. A few years later she attempted suicide. She has never recovered.

After the fire Maureen continued her family and work duties but as time went on she became moody, depressed and could not sleep. Her husband and she fought frequently. Often she had nightmares and screamed out and ran out of the house at night. Her husband finally left her and she moved to another area of the country with her three year old daughter. Shortly after, she started frequenting bars and when the neighbors reported her for child neglect, she was court-ordered to seek counseling. To keep her child she got help but struggled for years. However she turned her life around with the help of medication, Alcoholics Anonymous, and group meetings at her church. Several years later she was finally symptom-free and off medication.

Would immediate treatment of PTS symptoms have lessened Maureen and Janet's symptoms and therefore changed their lives? Research now indicates that it might well have helped. I wish we could have given them a chance to chose a different path soon after their traumas occurred. Both barely escaped with their lives in the forest fire. Both experienced PTS as a result. Neither received immediate treatment when they returned home, and both developed severe PTSD over time.

Milder PTS symptoms generally decrease soon after the trauma and gradually disappear. However, through no fault of yours, you may get stuck in the "on" position or be triggered again later. Maybe this metaphor will help you understand what happens when your body gets trapped in trauma mode. Picture the doorbell on your front door. You hear the doorbell ring and go to the door, but nobody is there. You expect the bell to stop, but it keeps on ringing. By now it's obvious the bell is stuck. You try to stop it, but it just keeps ringing. You try to ignore it as long as you can, but your family and neighbors are staring at you. Some even call out, "Can't you do something about that doorbell?"

You dash to your toolbox, grab a toolkit, and dash back to your door. You try to repair the bell, but you don't know how. Frustrated, angry, and agitated at the constant noise in your head, you might even hit the bell with a hammer. Now you have a broken doorbell, probably even a broken door, but the bell still keeps ringing. Why did **your** doorbell get stuck and not your neighbor's? Who knows? Stuff happens. But now your only options are to let the doorbell keep on ringing, or to accept that it's broken and find a skilled repairman to fix it.

WHERE DOES THE DIAGNOSIS OF PTSD ORIGINATE?

Whenever we hear the term PTSD in the media, it is usually associated with combat troops in war, rarely with accidents, abuse, or natural disasters. And to some degree, the reporters are right. During World War I the U. S. military first recognized the cluster of symptoms now called PTSD. Back then the disorder was called "shell shock." After World War II, it became known as "combat stress disorder" or "combat fatigue."

As time went on, researchers and psychologists realized that *any* person might respond to sudden, severe, and unusual stress in a way similar to soldiers in battle. The condition became known as Post Traumatic Stress Disorder, and in 1980 was added to the American handbook used to diagnose psychological problems, *The Diagnostic Statistical Manual, Third Edition* (*DSM-III*), in the "Anxiety Disorders" category. In the recently released *DSM-V*, PTSD is listed under a new category, "Trauma and Stressor Related Disorders."

What types of trauma can cause PTS or PTSD?

Here is a list of the types of trauma that cause PTS or PTSD. (Of course, these will not all pertain to you directly.):

- Experiencing or witnessing **a natural disaster**, including diseases, volcanoes, earthquakes, forest fires, hurricanes, tornadoes, tsunamis, and severe flooding, such as has taken place in New Orleans, New York, Boulder, Colorado and Haiti. Most of us think of these natural disasters as acts of God, entirely out of our control.
- Experiencing or witnessing **an accident,** such as a serious car accident, plane crash, house fire, or collapse of a building. We think of these as manmade disasters. However, most of us can understand that accidents are part of life and no one meant them to happen. Firemen, policemen, and first responders are included in this category.
- Experiencing or witnessing **a premeditated tragedy.** This category includes murders, child abuse, sexual and physical assaults, rapes, school shootings,

What types of trauma can cause PTS or PTSD?

kidnappings, torture, bombings, war, and terrorist attacks, like the one many of us remember on September 11, 2001 and now in California and Florida. These tragedies are becoming more frequent all around the world. People such as policemen, and soldiers are included in this category.

Take a guess as to which of the three types of trauma tend to create symptoms of PTS and PTSD most frequently and severely. If you guessed premeditated disasters, you are correct. This is quite logical. Nature has normal cycles of storms, disease, and earth movements. Accidents happen. But most of us can find few excuses for people who have deliberately killed or injured someone else, except in self-defense. In a premeditated tragedy, your loved one's death or your own injuries were intentionally inflicted and could have been prevented.

I believe there is a fourth category of tragedy, often ignored, though more frequently mentioned today than in the past:

Secondary PTS: This condition affects people who did not actually experience or witness the trauma in person, including military personnel not directly engaged in battle, first responders like emergency personnel, police officers and firemen, clinicians who work with PTSD survivors. They see the results of the trauma—often the blood and suffering—even though they didn't experience it firsthand. Another group of secondary PTS sufferers, often overlooked, may well be the loved ones of those who have been injured or killed, such as parents, spouses, children, and friends who imagine the traumatic event. The human mind is very powerful and may well be able to construct mental images of traumas so vivid that they affect the emotions and bodies.

Let's take war as an example. Since the media is saturated with graphic depictions of war and violence, it is fairly easy for civilians, especially close loved ones such as wives and mothers to imagine in excruciating detail what combat is like for their loved one: the constant danger, the improvised explosive devices (IEDs), the bombs exploding nearby, loved ones suffering injuries, the sounds and smells of the battlefield. In my experience working with family members, these images can indirectly trigger secondary PTS.

Although these people are usually not considered in the DSM as trauma survivors I would also like to mention people who have seen their mates, children, or family members die unexpectedly, even though the death occurred from an illness such as a sudden heart attack or a ruptured aneurism. I had a client who saw her mother suddenly bleed out from leukemia when they were shopping. Her symptoms were very similar.

How often does PTSD occur?

According to statistics the rate of PTSD among the general population is about 6.8%. It does not however single out people with traumas and the percentage of people who have PTSD due to a trauma. Survivors of trauma such as rape, sexual abuse, and combat have a rate of PTSD as high as 20-30%. About a quarter of all women have been sexually assaulted and a quarter to a third of these may well have PTS or PTSD. Many of my clients with PTSD were suicidal. According to the military more veterans annually than are killed in war, die by suicide.

What qualifies as an unusual and/or severe trauma?

The *Diagnostic Statistical Manual* (*DSM-IV*) defines severe and unusual trauma as an incident outside the realm of ordinary human experiences, such as simple bereavement, chronic illness, family conflict, or economic loss. (Of course, many of the symptoms of PTS can occur with these "usual" traumas as well, and the steps to recovery that follow are just as helpful to those people.) **Regardless of how other people classify an event, ultimately the trauma is severe and unusual if you perceive it that way.** The stressors I am talking about mostly in this book are usually sudden and cause intense fear, terror, and helplessness; a total loss of control; powerlessness; and a feeling that there is no safe place.*

Is it any wonder that many people will do almost anything—including becoming violent, avoiding reminders of the trauma, and denying they have a problem—in order to regain feelings of control and safety? To regain a sense of control, people may respond by withdrawing or becoming angry and aggressive. These responses are prompted by fear—a perfectly understandable emotion, but which nonetheless needs to be addressed. Ask yourself, "What am I afraid of?" The answer will assist you in finding a solution to your individual situation.

What Qualifies as an Unusual and/or Severe Trauma?

The greater the number of the five senses involved in the incident, the more powerful the effects. Although we often remember sights and sounds, we tend to forget that smell, taste, and touch can be just as powerful and multiply the impact of an event. According to research, smell is often the most powerful trigger. For example, the scent of roses may mentally transport a person back to a mother's funeral. A man who worked in the vicinity of the Twin Towers when the planes crashed into them on September 11, 2001, remembers seeing the fireball and hearing the terrifying explosion. He also remembers the acrid smell of the smoke and the taste and feel of grit in his mouth. The acrid smell most often caused him to relive the events of 9/11 in his mind.

In the course of my work, I noticed that much of the seriousness and severity of a trauma depended on the person's own **perception** of what occurred. So think for a minute. What were you taught as a child? About life? About death? What have your religion and culture taught you? How significant was the event to you? For some of you, the trauma may have mirrored events from your past that you thought were severe, even though others might not have seen the event in the same way. Only you can define for yourself how severe a trauma was or was not. To determine for yourself how severe your trauma was, ask yourself, from 1-10, how severe did you see your trauma to be?

A military officer who served in Afghanistan told me a story of finding the body of a young boy blown apart by an IED. With a heavy heart, the officer wrapped the body, knelt down, said a prayer, saluted, and buried the boy. Another soldier with him reacted very little to the same event. Why the difference? The officer thought it might be because he was married and had a little boy about the same age as the dead child. He understood what it would be like to lose a child. The nineteen-year-old soldier had no similar attachments.

If something important to you is suddenly lost, or if you believe something exists but then it is gone, you may feel intense fear, insecurity, vulnerability, and grief. This is what happened to many Americans after the terrorist attacks on the World Trade Center. Up to that time, we had felt safe in the United States, as if no one from outside could harm us. We were in control. But when the terrorists blew up the Twin Towers, suddenly our sense of security was shattered. Our security had been an illusion, but our belief that we were secure had kept us from feeling fear. When that belief disappeared, we clung to our government to make us feel safe again, even though that was impossible.

With terrorist attacks in California and Florida, and all over the world at this time, the fear has escalated almost to the point of hysteria and more and more people are willing to give up their values, their moral and religious beliefs as well as their freedoms, so they can feel safe and in control.

Some time ago I asked my father, a dedicated Christian man, "How did you and the other refugees in your group survive with your beliefs and values intact?" He said, "We were just as scared as anyone else but we took time to think it through and we didn't act on our fear. We kept our faith that God would be with us and lead us." He wiped away tears.

"**Be careful Anna. Don't let your freedom's go just because you are afraid.**"

Are some people more vulnerable to PTS and PTSD than others?

Although everyone is vulnerable to stress and susceptible to PTS, some people are more prone to it than others. Why? Mostly because of their genes. That's not their fault, and it isn't anything they can change.

Why do some people experience more severe stress reactions than others? While some people do not seem to be affected by prolonged stress after a trauma and return to feeling normal shortly after the stressors abate, depending on their environments and particular nervous systems and brains, they may be more susceptible to stress.

Interestingly, researchers have found that people who have been genetically gifted with the strongest memories are also more vulnerable to PTSD. A recent study by a neuroscientist at the University of Basel, Switzerland, discovered some people have a genetic signature that gives them the ability to form stronger memories. After studying 347 refugees of the Rwandan genocide, researchers found a clear indication that stronger memories were linked to a heightened risk of PTSD, often doubling the risk.

Recent research also indicates that women are more prone than men to develop PTSD, possibly twice as often. Why?

At this point we don't know, although functional MRI studies by Daniel Amen have shown that female brains function somewhat differently from men's brains in certain respects. Also, a woman's social and cultural environment differs from a man's. So it would not be surprising that men and women might react differently to stress as well.

The strength and severity of PTSD is also linked to genetic causes like genetically transmitted mental disorders, such as bipolar disorder, schizophrenia, or inherited depression. These can reduce your ability to deal with stress. Although gene variations for stress vulnerability are primarily inherited at conception, researchers are now finding that environmental factors, especially when experienced early in life (even in the uterus), can create changes in the body that permanently alter the susceptibility to stress. Thus, childhood trauma and/or abuse and neglect has a lasting effect not just on the mind but also on the DNA.

Epigenetics (on top of genetics) is a science that has just recently emerged. As scientists delve more into our DNA, researchers such as Bruce Lipton, are discovering that signals from our environment can actually create external modifications to DNA that turn genes on or off. Environmental factors influence how genes express themselves and how cells read genes. Scientists are now discovering these gene changes can be inherited by the survivor's children and by their children. They are calling it Inherited Trauma. This is particularly disturbing knowing the number of adults and children in the world who at this time are experiencing war, natural disasters such as floods and fires, shootings and accidents. Some scientists believe these changes can be passed on to the offspring. However, the environment does not change the DNA sequence.

A study conducted at McGill University in Quebec revealed DNA modifications that made people who were physically and/or sexually abused as children more sensitive to severe stress as they grew up. In certain people, the number of cortical hormone (stress hormone) receptors had actually been reduced. Although the research subjects were studied for abuse only, it is likely that any child growing up under prolonged, severe stress, such as in an alcoholic or violent family or neighborhood, or with a parent suffering from a severe emotional disorder, may experience similar changes in how he or she reacts to stress as an adult.

Researchers have found that biochemistry is also important. The fetal stress response of a child in the womb is a biochemical reflection of the mother's stress condition and her nutrition, as well as medications that she is taking. Also poisons in her food, water, and air, change stress susceptibility. As a result, children subjected to stress in the womb bear a biochemical tendency to react more strongly to stress in the future.

Other factors in stress susceptibility are learned. As I have mentioned, certain beliefs and values you were taught in the past affect your perceptions of what happens to you in the present. If you perceive you are more susceptible to stress than the people around you, remember, you are not at fault. And you are not alone. There are many, many people who may have these same vulnerabilities. Don't give up. Be cautious with medication, but don't rule it out. These are, at least in part, physical disorders that often can, in conjunction with psychotherapy, be successfully treated with a balancing chemical, the way insulin balances diabetes.

From my readings and experience of working with people who have PTSD, I've learned that the longer, more severe, or more continuous the stress, or the more frequently it occurs (such as in war and abuse), the more likely it will become unmanageable. The person never feels safe, and the mind and body can take only so much stress before they malfunction. Once he or she regains control over life, the stress fades.

Prolonged stress can lead to the dysregulation of the sympathetic nervous system which governs functions not under our conscious control (like breathing). If a person is experiencing a constant state of arousal, the nervous system can get stuck in the "on" state. As I mentioned earlier, I compare it to a stuck doorbell or a stuck horn on the car. The doorbell and the horn each have a very useful function, but they become irritating and disruptive if they won't stop. Just so, the "freeze, fight, or flight" response is essential to alert us to and help us escape from danger, but it becomes dysfunctional if it won't stop after the threat is gone. When this system does not later recalibrate to a normal level, PTS or PTSD can occur and the person begins to experience symptoms such as restlessness, nightmares, and hyper-vigilance.

Research has found that military personnel are predisposed to developing PTSD as a result of their training. Military training is generally geared to shutting down or cutting off thoughts and emotions in a time of crisis. If you are a veteran, you have been taught to be a machine that reacts instead of acts, and kills on command or whenever you perceive danger, without thought. You must flip into survival mode and shoot in order to save yourself and others. While this automatic reaction is necessary in combat, it makes life a lot more difficult after you come home. It is not easy to erase your training and relearn to take a moment of thought before you respond to a situation.

Other studies indicate that a lack of understanding from others plays a role in the increased likelihood of PTS or PTSD. This lack may take the form of others accusing you of feigning your symptoms or failing to understand what you are going through. Perhaps they believe in the old school of "hard knocks" and say or imply that your trauma is not severe, or is simply a case of bad nerves. They may advise you to "just buck up and get over it." The more people in your life who downplay or disrespect your experiences, the greater your stress and the more severe your PTS reaction.

So, yes, there are people who are more vulnerable to stress than others, but if you are one of them, the steps in Part 2 can help you. You can't control your genetics or your past environment, but you can **learn** ways of coping with situations that will lessen their impact considerably and help you become resilient and return to normal functioning. When you use these strategies, you will be able to change your stress level at any time you wish. Eventually you will feel back in control of your mind, emotions, and body, and your symptoms of stress will decrease.

What are the symptoms of PTS and PTSD?

PTS AFFECTS THE BODY, EMOTIONS, mind, and spiritual life. Are you having problems sleeping? Do you jump at noise? Are you hyper-vigilant, watching for trouble? Depressed and anxious? Maybe harboring unacknowledged thoughts of suicide? Do you relive the traumatic event during nightmares or flashbacks? Are you easily agitated, argumentative, or explosive with your family, mate or children? Do you isolate yourself? Are you using drugs and/or alcohol to cover your feelings and pain? **Even if you have only some of these symptoms, you may have PTS. Depending on how severe your symptoms are, you may well have the more severe PTSD.**

The following symptom list was compiled using the *DSM-IV* as a reference. This list is used by therapists to determine whether a person suffers from PTSD. Symptoms of PTS would be milder. For example, a PTS sufferer will probably not have flashbacks, though he or she may well have nightmares and sometimes vivid memories, but not as frequently as with PTSD.

Are these symptoms universal? No one seems to be sure. Some of the symptoms of PTSD I will discuss are more

What are the symptoms of PTS and PTSD?

prominent in some countries than others. When rescue workers and physicians come to help third world countries after a severe trauma such as an earthquake or war, the symptoms that survivors most often exhibit are the physical ones such as racing heart-beats, raised blood pressures, tensed and painful muscles, shaking, nausea, sweating, indigestion, and more frequent illnesses. They also seem most affected by the social disruptions that have occurred due to the traumatic event, and the loss of support they once had and need.

Some people believe these symptoms are actually different than in western cultures. Others believe, as I do, that the bodies of all humans react in a similar way, but because much of their time is spent trying to survive (food, shelter, etc.) the emotional and mental aspects of the individuals in these countries are less frequently acknowledged. Survivors may not be aware of their emotional and mental issues and may be much more conscious of the physical and social problems they are experiencing. Therefore these symptoms are not acknowledged or perceived in the way they are in more educated and affluent countries where survival after a trauma is usually assured.

PTSD SYMPTOMS IN THE TRAUMATIZED PERSON:

1. Has memories, flashbacks, or nightmares of the event. Some people may actually feel they are reliving the trauma, or they may have intrusive recollections of the event through sudden memories and dreams. For many, the events seem real at that moment, and they literally believe they are back in the experience.

A client I will call Barbara, a teacher at the local elementary school, started having flashbacks of her stepfather sexually assaulting her when her own daughter turned five. This was the same age she had been when her own abuse occurred. When triggered by her daughters screams or tears she would flash back to the past. She believed that she was literally being taken into her father's study and gagged to stop her from screaming and alerting her mother. According to Barbara's husband she would fall down, struggle, kick and try to scream. But her screams were silent as if she were still gagged.

Another example was Robert, a powerful warrior honored for his bravery in Vietnam and Panama. He felt life was meaningless and boring when he returned home. In order to feel useful and excited about life again, he joined the police force.

One night about eight years after he left the Marines, he was sent on a drug raid with his partner and a couple of other policemen. Before they knew what was happening, one of the criminals held a gun to Robert's partner's head. Just that quickly, he was mentally back in Vietnam. Without thinking, Robert lunged for the man. The first thing he remembered was other police officers shouting at him to stop. When he came back to reality, he saw he had shoved a gun into the drug dealer's throat and almost shot him. Robert left the police force soon after the incident. Although this was the first flashback he had experienced since combat, he was afraid it might happen again. The flashbacks continued for years, but after therapy and intense work on himself, Robert is doing well.

What are the symptoms of PTS and PTSD?

2. Has intense bodily fear reactions (racing heart, tensed muscles, shaking, nausea, sweating, indigestion, etc.) Heart arrhythmias are very common among survivors of trauma and many fear they are having heart attacks. These physical symptoms can occur when a person with PTS is exposed to an event that triggers memories of the trauma, or even some small aspect of it. The stimulus or trigger places the person back into the trauma. Even the mere anniversary or a movie portraying a similar event can re-traumatize a person. As an example, many veterans who viewed the movie *Saving Private Ryan* experienced flashbacks and nightmares.

3. Deliberately avoids the trigger(s) and numbs out or dissociates to avoid pain. PTS sufferers attempt to avoid places, thoughts, feelings, and situations that remind them of the trauma, or trigger flashbacks. Jack, introduced in Part 1, stopped working, then hid in his house so he would not hear the sounds that took him mentally back to his firefighting days. Some people have gone as far as to move into isolation such as the mountains or into the forest, away from civilization, to try to evade the things that will trigger flashbacks. Sometimes people feel detached from others and are no longer interested in life or in the things they enjoyed previously. Some feel numb, with little ability to feel emotions such as intimacy or tenderness. For others, even anger is absent. Many feel depressed and have a very limited sense of the future. My father, who lived with PTS most of his life, frequently said, "I won't live that long." He lived to be eighty-eight.

4. Has sleeping problems. People with PTSD experience increased arousal and anxiety that make it difficult for them to relax and fall or stay asleep. These people are constantly on "red alert" and overly watchful. A person with PTS feels jumpy, is easily startled, and feels as if he or she is in imminent danger. Although some think of these symptoms as a sleep disorder, many doctors now look at them as an anxiety disorder. Even after therapy has decreased symptoms considerably, sometimes the sleep disorder continues. Neuropsychologist, Dr. George Lindenfelt, believes this is an indication that the neuronal network remains activated.

5. Can have difficulty concentrating or finishing what he or she started. This perceived lack of follow-through creates problems in relationships, work, and school. One of my clients said that she felt as if her mind was in a fog, always split in pieces, some in the present and some in the past. Even though she tried, she could never get rid of the fog long enough to find all the pieces and put them back together. It has been found that dementia is more common in survivors in later life.

6. May have minutes of lost memories, or details of certain parts of the memories that cannot be retrieved. People may even forget important parts of the incident. When Andrea was hit by a car on her walk, she was tossed several feet into the air and landed on some rocks. She was diagnosed with Traumatic Brain Injury and later with PTSD. When I asked her what had happened, she said she remembered nothing between the accident and her arrival at the hospital.

What are the symptoms of PTS and PTSD?

The ambulance driver, however, said Andrea had remained conscious throughout the entire process. The loss of memory might be due to the brain injury, but it might also be due to Andrea's mind not wanting to remember.

Researchers at the University of Colorado at Boulder are now saying that they may soon be able to explain the techniques that the brain uses to wipe out unwanted memories, like severe traumas. What they are discovering is that the conscious mind can literally say "no" to remembering certain events after they happen. Is this the brain's incredible way of protecting us from traumatic memories we cannot deal with at that time? Whether these memories can be retrieved later is still not known.

7. May become irritable when he or she fears loss of control of a situation or person, or may actually become aggressive with unpredictable explosions of rage. Remember that rage comes from fear, especially fear of your life being out of your control. Everything is uncertain and you feel your life depends on you getting back some power to be able to feel safe and sane again. I think this fear of loss of control is the major issue for humanity. Whenever you are afraid, ask yourself, "What am I afraid of losing?" The answer is usually, "Loss of power and control." You think, "I can't control what others do, say, or think, or what will happen to me next." If people are honest, everyone fears this loss, but after a severe trauma these fears magnify and seem much more threatening. What will happen next? Will my family die or leave me? Will I lose my job? Will my country be attacked? To regain a sense of control, people often think that if they can make things happen exactly as they want them to, they will regain control over their lives. Of course that isn't true. Often by trying to control others we only push them away and create the very situation we fear.

So what *can* you control? Only you: your thoughts, your actions, and reactions—and sometimes those only tentatively. When the "freeze, fight, flight" response takes over you react from the emotional brain and you can no longer think with your logical brain

So you see, it is essential to retrain your brain to switch on logical thought before you act. If you fear hurting someone else, please seek help immediately.

8. **Suffers more frequent illnesses.** If the trauma occurred some time ago, you may have suffered more illnesses than usual since the event. People with PTS are left with a body on permanent high alert, sometimes for days, months, or years. While at one time it might have saved your life, in the long run, extended stress destabilizes the human autoimmune system. In many cases people with PTS and PTSD have underlying deep anger which has been correlated with cardiovascular disease and tumorigenic changes.

When you are under stress, the stress hormone cortisol floods your body. A continued and prolonged increase in cortisol eventually breaks down cells and affects every organ, degrading the immune system and making you more vulnerable to disease. The body pumps out too many immune cells called cytokines, which attack you rather than protect you.

What are the symptoms of PTS and PTSD?

9. Shows signs of depression and anxiety.

a) Depression:
If you are not sure whether you are depressed, please read the following questions and answer them truthfully.

1. Has anyone told you that you seem depressed, distant, and apathetic much of the time? *yup*

2. Have you lost interest or pleasure in most activities and people, and prefer to isolate? *indeed*

3. Have you had a significant weight loss or gain, or decrease or increase in appetite? *yup*

4. Do you suffer from insomnia, or sleep too much most nights? *not any more*

5. Do your muscles twitch or move too slowly? *yup*

6. Are you fatigued and low on energy? *yup*

7. Do you feel worthless or guilty much of the time? *yup*

8. Are your thoughts mostly negative? *yup*

9. Do you have difficulty thinking clearly, concentrating, or making decisions? *some time*

10. Do you often think about dying or suicide? *who doesn't*

If you have these symptoms or feel suicidal, please seek help with a counselor or medical doctor immediately. I will discuss steps you can take to help decrease your depression in Part 2.

b) Anxiety:
Until 2014, PTSD was classified as an anxiety disorder in the *DSM-IV*. Since then it has been reclassified under "Trauma and Stressor Related Disorders" in the *DSM-V*.

The following are the most common symptoms of anxiety:

- Motor tension issues: (a) trembling, twitching, or feeling shaky; (b) tense and sore muscles; (c) restlessness and fatigue
- Autonomic nervous system hyperactivity: (a) shortness of breath or smothering sensations; (b) accelerated heart rate; (c) sweating, dizziness; (d) nausea, stomachache, diarrhea, dry mouth; (e) flushes or chills; (f) frequent urination; (g) trouble swallowing or "lump in throat"
- Hyper-vigilance: (a) feeling on edge; (b) exaggerated startle response; (c) difficulty concentrating or "mind going blank"; (d) trouble falling or staying asleep; (e) irritability
- Anxiety sufferers describe their symptoms as comparable to those after drinking too many cups of coffee or caffeine-containing sodas.

10. Abuses drugs and alcohol. It is common for people with PTS to resort to using legal or illegal drugs and alcohol to

WHAT ARE THE SYMPTOMS OF PTS AND PTSD?

help them numb their feelings and pain. In recent years patients have been prescribed drugs by physicians to reduce anxiety, depression, and sleeplessness, and to stop physical pain. We are very fortunate to have these drugs, but some people have learned to rely solely on them to relieve their symptoms and have become addicted instead of investing in real recovery. With the easy access to prescription drugs at this point in our history, it is more and more common to have what is called "accidental suicides." Both Michael Jackson and Prince are said to be examples.

One of my clients credited alcohol with actually saving her life. Of course, knowing what drinking and drugs do to people, I was skeptical. She explained that the only way she had survived after being beaten and sexually abused by her boyfriend was to drink and take drugs. She was sure she would have killed herself if she had had no way out of the physical and emotional pain at the time. But her addictions created many more problems than they solved. She lost her friends, her two young children, and her job. In the end, to survive, she stopped drinking and taking drugs, sought therapy, and joined both Alcoholics and Narcotics Anonymous.

11. Experiences feelings of guilt and shame or self-blame. Some people call this guilt a "soul pain." I will further address the issue in the section on spirituality in Part 2.

12. Has suicidal tendencies. Many people who have had a severe trauma get more and more anxious and depressed and start to think of committing suicide many times a day. Some even have a plan. Men more often use guns and women an overdose of drugs. When I worked with suicidal people I found that most of them did not really want to die. They just wanted desperately the physical and/or emotional pain to end. And they couldn't see any other way out.

13. Has difficulty trusting others, and often questions God. It is normal and human to question. If you believe in God, at first you may have been enormously grateful that God spared your life, but then doubts appear. What kind of a God would have allowed this to happen?

For many years Mother Teresa lived amid continuous trauma and its effects, working as a missionary and healer in India. I used to wonder how she could continue trusting God after all she saw. I was sure I wouldn't be able to, under similar circumstances. After her death, a section of her journal was released to the public that revealed her doubts and struggles. Was there a loving God? Who was this God? Knowing Mother Teresa had grappled with the same issues the rest of us humans do, made me admire her courage that much more.

If these symptoms begin to interfere with your relationships, your serenity, and your daily functioning, you are likely experiencing PTS. Many people keep their inner turmoil secret and begin to isolate themselves. Don't. Regardless of who you are, female or male, reactions to severe stress are normal and predictable. But PTS can quickly worsen into a Disorder if you don't do something to alleviate the symptoms now. Help is available.

What happens in the brain and body during PTS?

HERE IS A SIMPLE DRAWING of the parts of the brain to explain how trauma, stress, and PTSD work. Of course the brain is not nearly as simple as I'm making it, but this diagram will help you understand the causes of some of your symptoms, and that they are normal for the type of trauma you have experienced.

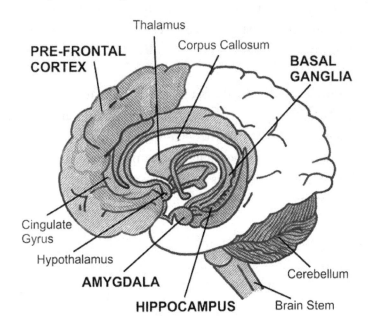

Limbic system=amygdala + hippocampus: A group of interconnected structures that mediate emotions, learning, and memory.

Amygdala: Center of emotions. Controls fear response and determines level of threat. It processes reflexive and instinctual emotions (the survival instincts) like fear and anxiety. Learning and memory are activated here as well. In brain imaging research, scientists have found that severe stress lowers the threshold of the amygdala's response to fear stimuli and thus reacts more severely.

Hippocampus: Plays a significant role in the formation of long term memory. Neuroscientists are finding that the hippocampus sometimes is smaller in people with PTSD than in other people. Of course it's a chicken or egg issue, but some think it may be due to continued severe stress responses in the brain.

Prefrontal cortex: The thinking part of the brain that controls impulses, attention span, focusing, organizing, and follow-through. Believed to be the area of the brain that developed last in evolution, the prefrontal cortex plans, sets goals, judges priorities, and allows us to suppress troubling memories and thoughts.

Basal ganglia: These control the body's "idling speed." When the basal ganglia are overactive, anxiety, panic, fearfulness, and conflict avoidance are often the result.

What Happens in the Brain and Body During PTS?

Remember, the brain is a physical organ just like your heart, your lungs, or your kidneys. Its purpose is to regulate the emotions, thoughts, memories, and nervous system. As soon as a real or imagined threat is perceived either consciously or unconsciously, as in PTS, your brain chemistry changes and the levels of adrenaline, norepinephrine, and cortisol increase. The brain's chief emotional center, the amygdala, which carries the survival instincts and reflexive emotions such as fear and anxiety, is activated. It tells you how to react to a situation before you have conscious thought. The amygdala also keeps track of all your past good and bad feelings about memories, but not the facts such as names, time frame, and location.

That is the job of the hippocampus. The hippocampus keeps track of the facts, but not the feelings, and plays a significant role in the formation of long term memory. Then, if need be, it sends these facts on to the prefrontal cortex, or thinking part of the brain, to plan, set goals, and judge priorities. If the hippocampus is overwhelmed by stress hormones, it loses the ability to separate time, and during a flashback you actually believe "then" is "now."

When the automatic, inborn survival instinct called the "freeze, fight or flight response" is activated by a real or perceived threat, the body directs most of the oxygen and blood to the brain stem and amygdala (emotional brain), not to the hippocampus and the prefrontal cortex that modulate the amygdala. The alarm sounds for only a thousandth of a second before the amygdala takes command and shuts down the hippocampus and the prefrontal cortex. The shut-down happens so quickly that there is no time to assess the threat logically. The body freezes for a moment, then fights or runs. Watch a frightened deer. It freezes, then darts away. It is believed that this temporary immobility allows the body to marshal enormous energy before it acts.

The amygdala sends panic messages into the rest of the brain, especially to the hippocampus. It becomes hyperactive and sears fragments of memory onto the mind with a force that's hard to extinguish. When a trigger in the present, such as a noise or smell, is associated with a past trauma, the past event reignites in the present, taking the shape of nightmares and flashbacks. Remember the early behavioral studies Pavlov performed on dogs? The researchers rang a bell, then gave the dog a treat. Soon all the researchers had to do was ring the bell and the dog began to salivate, even without the treat. That's how a gunshot may cause a PTS reaction such as a flashback, a memory, and a physical reaction. Your mind has paired the gunshot with danger from the past. Because of this intricate set of connections in the brain, the activation of one memory automatically triggers comparable memories and evokes similar feelings, both emotional and physical.

The amygdala has no way of tracking names, time, or place. However it remembers bad feelings as though they are occurring in the present. Flashbacks literally "flash you back" when something triggers a bad memory, even though you are safe in the present. Why has the brain evolved in this way? Think of the so-called good old days when all those lions and tigers and bears out there in a hostile environment were waiting to eat us for dinner. Over time, the human body developed a system to protect us from these threats. As the body evolved to help itself survive, it developed a nervous

What Happens in the Brain and Body during PTS?

system to alert people to danger. Adrenaline and cortisol, called stress hormones, are pumped into the organs, including the brain stem and the emotional centers in the brain, to increase the heart rate, make the breath come faster, tense the muscles, and make us alert and miraculously strong, ready to fight or run. But even now, so many years later, we have the same instinct. Some scientists believe that the brain has never adapted to sustain the pressures and stresses of modern life.

Normally, if the person escaped from the predator and the real or perceived threat ended, the adrenaline and cortisol levels receded to a balanced amount in the body. The sudden surges in chemicals, and then the return to a balanced state, both saved the person's life and actually helped the body tune itself up, just like when we take a car on a highway and run it at high speed.

Animals have a similar freeze, fight or flight system in their bodies and react to threats in similar ways to humans. If you watch *Animal Planet* on television, or Caesar Milan, or have read Temple Grandin's books, you will discover stories of severely abused dogs, or dogs in wartime, that contracted PTS and even PTSD. One such story involves a German Shepherd that helped soldiers find IEDs in Iraq. The dog was a great warrior, carefully selected and trained, and very successful in saving people's lives. But after encountering continued explosions for years, it lapsed into PTSD and was sent home. A year later it still shook, cowered, and hid, terrified of touch when triggered by certain noises. Does this sound familiar?

Contrary to how we often see ourselves, the physical body, emotions, and mind are not independent entities. All are irrevocably connected to the brain, a physical organ that maintains continuous close communication and feedback loops among the various elements. Without the brain, the body, emotions, and thoughts as we know them would not exist. Our thoughts and emotions are actually seated in distinct areas within the brain and are controlled by physical components such as hormones, enzymes, and proteins that are generated within the body.

In his book *Change Your Brain, Change Your Life*, Daniel G. Amen, M.D., describes how he used a brain SPECT (3-D imaging technique) to find that, compared to other people, a veteran with severe PTSD had markedly increased left-side activity in the basal ganglia (a collection of nuclei outside and above the limbic system). This type of basal ganglia activity is generally associated with chronic irritability or anger. Dr. Amen speculated that the veteran's thirteen-month war experience had set the basal ganglia to be on constant alert. The veteran had never learned how to reset his brain back to normal.

Usually when the threat is gone, the adrenaline and cortisol surges end and the brain resets itself. But in PTS the neuronal circuitry becomes frozen and the trauma memories are locked into the brain.

In some cases when a person has had to live under constant threat and crisis, as many veterans and people who have lived with family abuse, street violence, or war have, the body becomes addicted to the surges of adrenaline as it would to a drug, and craves to get back to that level of excitement (fear

What Happens in the Brain and Body During PTS?

and excitement create very similar effects in the body, which doesn't distinguish between them). Life becomes meaningless without that constant adrenaline rush. Many veterans feel useless when they come home, and sign up for another tour of duty or become policemen or emergency technicians in an effort to regain a sense of purpose. For example, one of the veterans I counseled became an FBI agent and worked undercover.

During the time of crisis, people become detached and live in denial of what might happen to them. With many of the people I treated for PTSD, I found that when their bodies believed they were no longer in danger, they began to release the emotions they had hidden in order to function during the event. People built firewalls around themselves while in constant trauma. At the time, the walls served them well. However, when they were safe, the walls collapsed. This is not an unusual occurrence for people experiencing prolonged trauma such as child abuse, domestic or neighborhood violence, or war. Just imagine what many of the refugees from the middle east may be experiencing after they are finally safe.

PART 2

Twenty Steps to Help You Heal

These steps to recovery have been placed in the approximate order you will need to practice them in order to heal. But you don't have to do all of them, or practice them in the order presented, if that doesn't serve you. For now, only practice those steps that you are drawn to and feel you need. Later you may wish to try some others as well.

The Healing Wall, Part II

by Patrick Overton, Ph.D. and Vietnam veteran

II.
I visited the Wall.
One evening in the late summer of the year,
when the cool winds blew across the Mall and the
early evening sun was crisp, I went to the Wall, again.
I stood where I had stood before but refused to go.
And without ever deciding,
without ever giving consent
I found myself moving toward it,
pulled by some force I would not see,
drawn by memories I could no longer deny.
I began the slow descent into the dark hole,
not wanting to but needing to go back into
what I had spent twenty-five years trying to forget.

Patrick Overton is a survivor of trauma during the Vietnam War. The Wall was a monument, a symbol, erected in Washington, DC, for those who died and those who survived. Here he speaks of his years of denial about what he had experienced before he could face his feelings and memories.

It's time to deal with your trauma.

As you can see from the poem "The Healing Wall," written by Vietnam veteran Patrick Overton, many people have a hard time honestly facing their traumatic experiences even years after they occurred. It is easier to pretend that the symptoms they've been having since the trauma don't hold any power over their everyday lives.

If you are like many other people, it is often your family and friends who see most clearly the pain and problems you are facing. Because they love you and want you to recover, they may also be the ones who confront you most often about the issues they have observed. Don't ignore them. Listen to them and carefully evaluate what they say to see whether they are right.

I understand that facing your issues takes a lot of courage, but you probably realize by now that running away from problems or pretending they don't exist won't work to improve your relationships, your job, or your emotional and physical health. According to the CDC about 85% of all physical illnesses are influenced by emotions.

Characteristics of a Resilient Person

Resilient people are like young, flexible trees. They can bend in a storm, but do not snap. Instead they spring back when the storm is over and keep growing.

Your goal in recovery will be to alleviate, or at least diminish, the symptoms of PTS that you have identified in the symptom list in this book. Now that you have recognized the feelings and behaviors that you no longer want in your life, it is time to look at what you need to learn to help you become more resilient to stress in the future.

Below I've listed some characteristics that researchers have discovered occur most frequently in resilient people who can comfortably deal with stress. To some degree these are genetic, but research also shows that you can cultivate these characteristics to master any crisis. Whether they are based in genetics or are learned over time doesn't matter. You can study and practice them now. Don't give up. You didn't learn to read and write in a day. Remember how many years it took you to develop your present patterns of behavior.

Characteristics of a Resilient Person

Here are some common answers:

- They stay connected to others.
- They are optimistic.
- They are spiritual.
- They are playful and enjoy themselves as children do. They wonder about things, experiment, and laugh.
- They pick their battles. They focus on things over which they have some influence and not on things they can't control.
- They give back to others.
- They stay healthy.
- They find the silver linings in problems.
- They gain strength from adversity.

What makes people happy?

Contrary to what many people in Western cultures often believe, researchers have found that what the majority of people around the world say makes them most happy is not having more things, but rather the quality of their social relationships.

The following are some of the common answers:

- Connection with people you love and a deep spiritual connection
- Novelty, change, or excitement
- A challenge that makes you stretch to the point where you experience the best of yourself
- Creative expression, such as art, music, gardening, or imagining new ways of doing something
- Meaning, purpose, and contribution: Do I matter? Have I contributed to this world? Before the trauma you may have felt you mattered. But now?

Following are twenty steps that will help you become more resilient even if you evaluate that your trauma was not very severe. They could change your life. Give them a try.

STEP ONE:
BECOME STABLE.

Before you move on to any other steps, please ask yourself whether you are stable and functional enough to be safe. If the answer is no, make an appointment with your physician, a psychotherapist, or your mental health center before you do anything else.

Flashbacks, nightmares, and vivid memories devastate trauma survivors emotionally. The intense fear that rips through their bodies when they are triggered (activated) to relive their traumas are incredibly hard to handle, but they are also the greatest motivators for change. You've heard the phrase, "No pain, no gain." I don't believe that the saying is true in all cases, but often it is.

When the event is triggered after the trauma, the amygdala or emotional center of the brain sends panicked messages to other areas in the brain, including the hippocampus, the brain's center for storing long-term memories. Past events reignite in the present and create intense memories, nightmares, and flashbacks. For some people these repercussions come several times a day; for others, weekly; for still others, rarely; but when they come, they may be strong enough to immobilize a person.

Until you are able to calm yourself and disengage enough from these emotional memories to make life manageable, it will be hard to practice any of the steps in this book. Although flashbacks rarely occur for people who have PTS (as opposed to PTSD), bad memories and nightmares are common. Please spend as much time practicing the suggestions in Step One as you need to feel some sense of control over your symptoms before moving on to the other steps.

As a person with PTS or PTSD, the biggest hurdle you face is to be able to separate the past from the present, so that you can see that your flashbacks or nightmares are merely memories and that you are safe now. Remember that the amygdala (emotional center) is being triggered. To bring you back to reality and into the present, you must learn to reactivate your prefrontal-cortex (thinking, reasoning center) in order to get in touch with the facts, time frame, and location of your current reality.

1. Program your mind. Your mind is literal and will gradually learn to believe whatever you tell it. Before you experience a flashback or dream, remind yourself frequently throughout the day, "I am not in ____ now. I am home (or wherever you are now.) I am safe," or any other reassuring words that help you feel safe. Repeat this frequently, so that your unconscious mind will begin to believe what you are saying. Say it out loud so you can literally hear your own words. Try this technique a hundred times a day. Place the words on file cards and tape them to your mirrors, dashboard, TV, etc., so you can read them wherever you go.

STEP ONE: BECOME STABLE.

2. Stop and think before you act. In an instant, your brain sizes up a situation. If it decides the situation resembles the trauma you experienced (by sight, sound, smell, taste, or feel) and that you are in danger, you experience intense fear. Your body reacts immediately by getting ready to fight or run. Your muscles tense, your heart races, and time seems to stand still. This process is like a feedback loop that happens so rapidly, most people are unaware of it.

First and foremost, you need to know that, as a child, you gradually learned that, rather than react immediately to a trigger, you needed to take a moment to allow the prefrontal cortex (logical brain) to assess your situation and then act. You learned to ask questions of yourself, such as, "Is this threat real?" If the answer was yes, you then asked, "What is my best course of action?" By the time you were an adult, you were able to control most of your impulses. But after a serious threat to you or someone you love, you may well revert back to survival responses of fighting or fleeing each time you are triggered.

When people have not learned impulse control or sometimes when terrified, they do what the old adage says: "Shoot first and ask questions later." If you were in the military or the police force, you were taught to override the prefrontal cortex and respond without thinking when in immediate danger. In an attack you probably would not have survived if you hadn't reverted to the automatic survival responses. But now that you are safe again, you will need to unlearn what you learned and retrain your brain to take a few seconds to assess the situation, come up with a solution, and then act (not react). It's not easy, but you learned it as a child, and you can do it again.

Here are some ways to help you retrain yourself to think before acting (fight or flight):

- Talk to yourself silently, or even out loud if you need to. Let your mind know, several times a day, that yes, you were in danger but you are safe now, that you have the time to think before you act.
- Usually people with PTS startle easily and react immediately. Observe yourself throughout the day. Whenever you jump, tell yourself, "STOP. THINK." Don't act immediately. Notice whatever startles you. Was it truly dangerous? What should you do about it? If it is nothing dangerous, tell yourself, "I'm safe. I'm all right. Relax." Then breathe in and out deeply and slowly at least three times, allowing yourself to relax. Continue with this practice whenever you feel startled, for as long as it takes to become less reactive.
- If you need to, substitute a sound for an automatic action. Making a sound will give your prefrontal cortex more time to think logically. For example, one of the adolescents I counseled tried to change his actions with thoughts alone, but was unable to stop when he felt threatened. Usually he raised his fists and punched before he could think. He realized that thinking alone wouldn't do the trick. He needed to substitute a different action for punching. So he learned to shout instead of punch (presumed threat—shout instead of punch). In the split second

Step One: Become stable.

it took to shout, his logical brain kicked into gear and he was able to stop the punch.

3. When you have a bad memory or feel yourself heading into a flashback. always first make sure that you are safe. Check around you. When you have determined you are safe, think through the trauma as if it were happening long ago, not right now. Teach your mind to separate the past from the present.

4. Using your logical brain, think through your body's typical first response that signals you're about to experience a flashback or vivid memory. Does your heart race? Do you sweat or shake? What do you feel as you head into a flashback? Make the thoughts clear in your mind. "I am shaking and sweating because I'm remembering that I was afraid during my traumatic experience three years ago. This is a memory." Understanding how your emotions and your body interact will sensitize you to your body's signals, eventually leading you to a point where you can control an oncoming flashback, or avoid it completely. If you don't yet recognize these physical signals, ask yourself after the flashback, "What happened first?" Usually your mind will tell you. If not, try to picture yourself standing outside of your body on a hill, watching your body below. What is your body experiencing? Gradually you will be able to separate yourself from the trauma long enough to recognize what your body does when your emotions sense a threat.

5. When you prepare for bed, repeat the words, "I am safe now. The trauma was in the past," several times before you go to sleep. Your mind is more powerful than you can imagine.

Ask your mind honestly to help you, and it will. But don't expect immediate results. Retraining your mind takes time.

Tell your mind before you go to sleep, "I am able to intrude on my dream with my waking mind and consciously change my dreams." In time the logical mind will be able to watch your dream while you are having it and make your emotional mind aware that you are safe and that the dream isn't real. At that point, you will usually wake up.

When you wake up go through the nightmare to make sense of it but then take time to revision it the way you wanted the dream to end. Take control of it.

6. Write down your memory, dream, or flashback and refer to it clearly as happening in the past. "It is just a memory." Distance yourself from it. Don't allow it to stay in your mind as though it's a reality now. "That was a year ago, March 25th at six p.m. in Central Park. I am not there now. Today is April 4th at 2 p.m. in New Mexico. I am home now. I am safe." Shift your attention outside of yourself. Look at your clothes. You are not in the same clothes you wore then. Look around the room and identify specific objects that are different than the things you saw when the trauma occurred. By thinking these thoughts, you are helping the hippocampus to engage.

Remind yourself that you survived. In her book *8 Keys to Safe Trauma Recovery*, well-known psychotherapist and trauma recovery specialist Babette Rothschild advises, "Write your epilogue first." What she means is that usually when people journal or talk about their trauma, they begin the story just before the actual event and then recount the details as they remember them happening. Often, however,

Step One: Become stable.

they get stuck somewhere in the middle of the trauma and never get to the end and beyond, all the way to the present. So the mind forgets they survived and keeps them "trapped" in the trauma. Rothschild advises that you begin the story in the present, or at a significant point after the trauma, and work back to the trauma. This approach will remind you that indeed you did survive.

7. If you are driving a car or working on dangerous machinery when you get a signal that you are about to go into a flashback or vivid memory, stop what you are doing and move to a place of safety. If you are somewhere where you can safely lie down on a sofa, a bed, the floor, or the ground, do so.

8. Immediately reassure yourself that you are not in the traumatic situation now and you are safe. Repeat several times, "I am home (or wherever). I am safe now. I survived." If you believe in a higher power, ask that power for help. Use your senses of sight, hearing, smell, sound, and touch to convince your mind you are not experiencing the trauma now. "I see the swing my kids play on every day. I see my neighbor's green car. I hear the sound of children playing. I smell soup cooking. I am touching grass. I am touching my jeans." Remind yourself that the flashback comes from the emotional brain, the amygdala, but you have a logical higher brain that can help you see that you are no longer there. Trust it.

9. After the dream or flashback, lean back and give your body permission to feel what it needs to feel. For example, let yourself shake and cry. The body has natural means of dealing with stress, and shaking is one of them. Tears are another. Have you ever watched your dog shake after a trauma? Or a child burst into tears after being frightened? We'll discuss these natural reactions in more depth later. For now, know that when you stop fighting against the natural reactions of your body and emotions, you lessen the stress.

10. For many people, breathing through the re-experienced trauma is very helpful. Close your eyes. Breathe slowly, steadily, and evenly, all the way in and all the way out, centering your thoughts on your chest and hearing the sound of your breath coming in and out. Feel your chest rise and fall. This deep-breathing exercise will help you relax enough to get to the other side without severe effects.

11. Find an object that helps you relax. Find a sea shell, a special rock, a polished stone, a ball, or anything else that you value and that centers and calms you. Keep it in your pocket and touch it often throughout the day when you feel relaxed, so you connect the object with a sense of being okay. As soon as you feel yourself slipping into a memory or flashback, touch the object and feel yourself relax. The object serves as an anchor to the real world, here and now.

12. Record calming music or a reassuring message on your smart phone. The message can be in your own voice or that of someone you love. Choose a sound that helps you stay in the present. Play it when you notice the first signs of a flashback and let the soothing words and voice bring your mind

Step One: Become stable.

back to the present. You can also create a calming CD or use calming music at night, before you go to sleep.

13. Use a nightlight if it helps to bring you back to reality after you wake up from a nightmare. Complete darkness can often trigger fear when you wake up and don't recognize where you are. Your mind believes there is someone out there threatening you. A nightlight can help you see your surroundings and remember you are safe at home.

14. If these guidelines don't work, ask for help from someone you trust who is likely to be present when nightmares or flashbacks occur, like your spouse or partner. Discuss with him or her how he or she can help you. For example, your partner could gently repeat, over and over if necessary, "You are home with me now. You are safe." If you can tolerate being touched, let the person hold you or touch your arm, centering you in the present. Ask her or him to repeat, "I am here. Hear my voice. Feel my hand. Look around you. See the bed, the table, the sofa. See the tree outside our window."

15. Always talk to your children about what is happening to you. Tell them how they can help you. If you do not become violent when you enter a flashback or nightmare, you might set up a family conference and tell them they can help you by touching you gently and saying, "Daddy, Daddy (Mommy, Mommy). We're home. I'm here." If you are afraid of becoming violent or hurting them in some way, you may want to tell them they need to leave the room when you signal them, that you will be okay, and you will come to get them when the memory is over. Always reassure them that this is about what happened to you and has nothing to do with them. It is not their fault. And things will get better but it will take time.

16. Instead of avoiding intimidating places altogether, slowly explore them in safety with someone you trust, like a mate or a friend. If you live or work in an environment that triggers you frequently, find ways to modify it without isolating yourself or leaving. You might use sound-dampening earphones, ear plugs, etc., to block out triggering noises. But if you can't stay, don't punish yourself. Leave, as Jack did when he left the fire department. Plan to re-expose yourself gradually and in a safe manner when you are ready to do so. (Check Step Eleven to learn about Prolonged Exposure Therapy.).

17. Be discerning about the books you read, the movies and TV programs you watch. When a mother I worked with, who witnessed her child's kidnapping, read a fiction book of a kidnapping she thought it would help her resolve what happened but instead she went right into a flashback and had difficulty recovering. So be careful. The mind is powerful.

Seeing violent images and hearing screaming may also trigger you unnecessarily. For example, many veterans experienced flashbacks while watching the movie *Saving Private Ryan*. I would suggest you only see a movie that might trigger you with someone present to provide immediate help, should you need it.

18. To get past the "freeze" response of your body, literally get moving. When you feel immobilized, move your legs

Step One: Become stable.

and arms, walk, run, do gentle exercises. Some people walk the mall or take a run in the park. Your mind will follow your body.

19. If you are really serious about recovery, don't carry firearms. If you do, keep the bullets or firing pin in a different pocket than your gun. Although it may be legal for you to carry a loaded weapon, until you are at a point where you can take time to assess a problem before you react, having immediate access to a loaded gun can put you and others at great risk. Depending on where you live, you will very rarely need a gun to protect yourself. Many people would not be spending the rest of their lives in prison if they had not had immediate access to a loaded weapon.

Statistics indicate that most people killed by gunshot wounds are loved ones mistaken for perpetrators and intruders or children who find the weapon and accidentally shoot themselves or someone they love. One of my first clients, a twelve year old boy, snuck his dad's gun from the glove compartment while his dad was in the grocery store, started playing with it, and accidentally shot and killed his younger brother who was sitting in the back seat. He could not forgive himself.

If you feel you absolutely need to carry a gun, don't load it and/or remove the firing pin. By the time you have loaded the weapon or replaced the pin, your logical mind will most likely be in control again. Still, it's a big risk. If you can manage to get along without a firearm, do so. Learn a martial art, use a horn or pepper spray instead. They are not lethal.

20. If you are stressed, take time to get away into nature and decompress.

For some ideas on this, check Step Fifteen.

Some counselors believe that you should deal with your memories and emotions immediately following a trauma. But until you feel stable enough to cope with them, this may not be the right time for you, and the memories may cause you to become even more dysfunctional. With time, you will be able to separate the past from the present and distance yourself from the memories enough so the mind and body won't react as if the trauma is occurring now. At that time, you can deal with the memories. In the meantime, if you feel compelled to talk about your memories, check Step Nine for some techniques to cope with memories and emotions.

STEP TWO:

Stay connected to other people and animals.

Few other steps are as important as this one. When Melissa was 17 years old she was driving her father's car to a party. She had asked her friend Natalie to come with her. When she returned a text from her boyfriend she veered into oncoming traffic and a large truck hit her car. Natalie died in the hospital two days later. Although Melissa had not been drinking she felt enormous guilt and shame.

So how did she react to this situation?

Like many others who have had a severe trauma, she began to isolate herself and stopped mingling with her friends. By the word "isolate" I don't mean moving into the mountains, far away from others. I am speaking more of mental and emotional withdrawal and isolation.

It is valuable to take time in nature from time to time, away from the hustle and bustle of the city, to decompress and listen to the birds and the trees in the wind, to go fishing and hiking. However, after a few days or weeks in nature, it will be time to return to civilization.

Even though you might feel like it, **don't isolate yourself**. Humans are social beings and need companionship and support. It's the way we evolved. We now know how very important it is for anyone—but especially survivors of trauma—to connect to others. According to recent research cited in Gabor Maté's book, *When the Body Says No*, people who have a good support system of friends and family with whom they can share feelings and activities are happier and become ill less frequently. Those without such a support system when under chronic stress exhibit suppressed immune systems and are often tired, ill, and/or depressed.

You need at least one close relationship with someone who cares about you, just the way you are, and with whom you can truly be yourself and share your innermost feelings and thoughts without being judged. People who maintain an impersonal distance from everyone may have many so-called "friends," but say they are lonely. Often the person you reach out to will be another person who has had similar experiences, because he or she understands what you have experienced and will actually "hear" you.

Reaching out to others takes a lot of courage, but most of you are familiar with what it takes to be courageous. Think back to a time when you were courageous. What happened? Usually it meant doing something you would rather not do, but you did it anyway. When my clients told me how hard it was to stay in touch with others, I would empathize with them, and then I would say, "If you really want to get better, do it anyway."

You are not a victim at present. You are an adult and you can choose in what direction you will go, up or down.

Here are some ways that will help you reconnect to others:

Step Two: Stay connected to other people and animals.

1. Find a companion you can trust and talk to about what is going on inside (either human or animal). Some people feel compelled to tell their story to an empathic ear immediately after the trauma. If this is you, look for someone you can trust who will not judge you, but will listen instead of giving advice. Research has shown that keeping secrets is unhealthy.

The act of keeping a secret about a traumatizing event can cause even more damage than experiencing the event itself. Have you ever heard the saying, "Confession is good for the soul?" Psychologist James Pennebaker, in a lengthy study, determined that when clients told their secrets, their health improved and measurable decreases in their stress hormone levels occurred.

If you don't have anyone to turn to, and you feel too vulnerable to talk openly with people, find an animal to talk to. Many of my clients developed close friendships with horses, dogs, cats, or even rabbits. They talked to them, told them their worst experiences, confided their dreams, and stroked and touched them. Regardless of what you say to an animal, it will love you and accept you. Regardless of what secrets you tell it, you will bond with each other. Bonding with an animal is a very important step that has even helped people decide not to end their lives. If you live somewhere you can't own a pet, consider volunteering at a nearby animal shelter.

One of my adolescent clients who had been sexually abused by her father spent time every day in the woods talking to a squirrel. He would come down the tree to meet her every day and he chattered away as she told the squirrel all her problems. Another client had a rabbit who knew all her secrets of abuse as a child. As an adult, she bought a stuffed rabbit that she felt symbolized her rabbit from her past, and she carried it with her to give her comfort. Sometimes I saw the rabbit's ears sticking out of the purse when she came in for sessions.

Recently I met a woman during a book signing for one of my novels. She asked me what I was currently writing. I mentioned this book and she smiled. "Wow," she said. "That's amazing. I work for an organization called Puppies Behind Bars. We teach prisoners to train dogs for disabled veterans, especially for veterans with PTSD." There are also several other organizations that train service dogs. For a bestselling, heartwarming book of stories about soldiers and their service dogs, read *Soldier Dogs* by Maria Goodavage.

Dogs especially make great companions and can help you through difficult times. One day I took my little dachshund, William Wallace (from *Braveheart*), out for a walk in our neighborhood. A large truck passed by. In it sat a tall, handsome young man in uniform, and on his shoulder, nuzzled next to his ear, lay a little sleeping poodle. When I returned home I mentioned the experience to my husband, who had served as a military officer when he was young. The first thing he said was, "Now that's a real man!"

2. Develop relationships with others, especially in groups who understand how you feel and with whom you can share your experiences and feelings. Hospice, 12 step programs, church groups, community groups, local VA or social services. Usually the group is moderated by a counselor and/or has steps to follow that keep you on track. You will be able

Step Two: Stay Connected to Other People and Animals.

to share your experiences and give and receive empathy and understanding, as well as great advice.

A note of caution: if you join a group that does not have a positive attitude or a positive leader, you may actually get more depressed and feel more and more hopeless. Leave the group if you feel that happening and find or form another group.

3. Use Skype or Face Time to keep in touch with your family and close friends. In many situations now, families and friends are scattered around the country and sometimes around the world. We are very fortunate to have Skype and Face Time, an inexpensive video-telephone service. These provide both visual and sound connections. Seeing your loved one's body language is actually much more revealing and bonding than just the voice alone. Staying in contact via these new technologies will help you stay close to the people whom you love and who love you the most, especially in these difficult times.

4. If you live in a rural location and have no support groups near you, find one on the Internet. There are several. If you have no computer, don't use that as an excuse. You may have access at your public library. Search for "PTSD support groups" in Google or another search engine. Evaluate several sites and their blogs before you decide on the one best for you. If possible join one in which members have had similar traumas as what you have experienced. Look for bloggers who have similar values to yours, who are empathic and good at listening, and whose writing makes you feel uplifted and encouraged.

5. Find a local group or organization you can join that has values and interests similar to yours. This can be a church, singles club, political party, chess club, Lions, Elks or Kiwanis Club, honors society, book club, photography club, writers' league, twelve-step programs, or any other group you find to be positive and that helps you become the person you want to be.

6. Many people after a severe trauma have resorted to drugs and alcohol to deal with their stress. If you have a drug or alcohol problem or are addicted, go to a local community or church recovery group, or to Alcoholics Anonymous (AA) or Narcotics Anonymous (NA). If your significant other has a drug or alcohol problem, attend a program for family and friends, like Alanon. You will find incredible support and wisdom in most of these groups. If you need to attend for a while before you begin to talk, that's okay. A sponsor can help you. Make sure to study and work on the twelve steps if you decide on AA or NA. These steps have helped millions of people overcome their addictions.

7. Get reacquainted with your family, significant other, and children again. If you have been **emotionally** and/or **physically absent** from your family, your family and children don't know you anymore, and you don't know them. Now that you are in recovery it is time to get reacquainted with each other.

Take a night out with your mate at least once a week, just the two of you. Do something you both enjoy, like seeing a movie or going out for dinner. Make sure you take time to talk and hold hands. Go back and reminisce about the good

Step Two: Stay connected to other people and animals.

times you had before the trauma. Remember why you fell in love and what you liked about each other. Both of you need to share what has happened inside yourself during the time after the trauma, if possible. Share your feelings and dreams for the future. Talk about what has changed. Talk about what you still have in common.

Sometimes it takes a third person to help moderate in a dispute. Find a minister or a counselor to help you. If possible, decide on a divorce or separation only after the two of you have undergone partner counseling.

8. Depending on your children's ages, you may need to start from the beginning. If you have been **physically absent** they may barely remember you, and they have adjusted to life with your spouse and without you. Follow her/his rules until you can work out new rules together. Don't expect the children to accept you or listen to you at first. You are a stranger to them. Maybe the only place they have seen you is in photographs and on Skype. You need to get to know each other before you can fully become a dad or mom again.

If you have been **emotionally absent you** will also need to start over. As with physical absence, get to know your children the way they are at this point in time, not as they were before the trauma. Ask your children what they like to do, what they think of daycare or school, what sports, TV shows, games, books, and toys they like. Take each child out separately and regularly, one-on-one, to do something they love to do. Interact with them even if you don't feel like it. If the children are learning to use the computer or ride a bike, join them and teach them or learn along with them. Teach them sports and games. Plan family outings regularly, and attend their recitals and sports events. Please keep the criticism and rules to a minimum. Give yourself permission to hold them close, listen attentively to their problems and joys, become playful again and have fun.

A mistake many people make after a severe trauma is to not let their children know what is going on. As a result, the experience traumatizes them as well. If you remember my personal story in the introduction, you will understand how your child may be feeling as well. Let your children know that when you have nightmares, get angry, or draw away from them, it's not their fault. Tell them in very general terms what happened to you and what is going on with you now, so they don't feel they are to blame for your trauma or the way you are reacting. Say something like, "Jimmy, this has nothing to do with you." Then give a short but honest explanation of what is happening. Let your partner help you when possible. Become a team.

9. As you become reacquainted with your children, set rational rules and consequences together with your spouse or partner, and support each other in your decisions. If you need to change the rules that have been set in your absence, or if you have become lax with rules because you were unable to deal with the stress in your life, try not to criticize each other in front of the children. Together decide what your rules will be as of now and follow through on the rules. They must know you are a team and that their parents are in charge. Children need limits and consistency, as well as love. It makes them feel secure.

Step Two: Stay connected to other people and animals.

10. Ask for help whenever you need it. Many people are ashamed or afraid to ask for help in case they will be rejected or thought of as weak. However, we live in community and need to depend on each other. If you ask someone for help and she or he says no, ask someone else. Don't give up.

Carefully select the people you will trust. Observe people first before committing to relationships with them. Check for these characteristics of a potential good friend: non-judgmental, empathic, a good listener, does not take advantage of others, open-minded, and centered. Most of all, watch that their actions match their words. Trust someone who says he or she will do something and then does it. Remember the politicians. Do you trust those who say one thing and then, a year or even a day later, say or do the exact opposite? Of course, don't forget, everyone is human and will sometimes make mistakes.

Remember: Love is freely given. Trust is earned.

STEP THREE:
Empower yourself.

1. Look at your positive attributes. When you are feeling depressed or anxious, most of your thoughts about yourself will be negative. What your mind is telling you is false. Your thinking is not accurate because of an imbalance of certain neuro-chemicals in your brain. In order to recover, you must create an equilibrium in your brain chemistry again. How do you do this? Antidepressants can help. But it is just as important, and longer-lasting, to think more positively about yourself and others.

Use your logical forebrain. The idea that you are only weak is irrational. If that were the case, you wouldn't have come this far in your life. Obviously you have many strengths. You just can't see them right now. According to a recent research study published in *Neuroscience Therapeutics*, it is important to look toward the future instead of dwelling on the past and on your current limitations. Develop skills that help you maintain positive expectations and a positive outlook. Choose to focus on the present and the future instead of the past. Here are some exercises to help you feel stronger, more confident, and more positive about yourself so you can take charge of your life again. Write down the answers to these exercises in

Step Three: Empower yourself.

a notebook so that you can reread them and add to them at a future date.

- Make a list of five of your strengths and virtues: (e.g., persistent, critical thinker, loving, courageous, cooperative, work for justice, loyal, responsible, wise, can laugh, creative). At first you may not come up with many strengths. After all, that's not the way your brain is thinking right now. I'll help you by asking you some questions. Do you love your friends and family? Loving others and yourself is the greatest strength you can have in this world. It ultimately creates peace in the family and the world. Have you helped anyone in your life? Have you ever stayed and faced your problems, or defended someone else by your words or actions, when all you wanted to do was run? This is courage. Have you done well in school, in sports, at a job?
- Write down any incidents you remember when you displayed these strengths and virtues, whether before, during, or after the trauma.
- What accomplishments are you proud of in your life? These don't need to be large achievements. Maybe you went to the mental health center to ask for help, or you have completed a project you started. Those qualify as accomplishments.
- Write down occasions when you helped someone else, or when you used your strengths and virtues for a purpose greater than your own goals.

- Focus on the things you have the power to change in your life, like your behavior and your thoughts. Write them down.

2. Count your blessings and change your attitude. I'm sure you have heard "count your blessings" before from well-meaning people such as parents, teachers, and religious leaders. But I am asking you to literally list your blessings on paper. I find the easiest way for me to do this exercise is to compare myself to other people in the world. It's amazing how rarely I felt depressed as a psychotherapist who saw eight clients daily, five days a week.

You might remember some of the people and countries you have seen in the news. What advantages do you have that they don't have? Did they have freedom of speech and religion? A good education? Health care? Safety? Enough food and decent lodging? My father's family, like many of our immigrant ancestors, fled their home and wealth, leaving everything behind for the privilege of being free.

Think of yourself as a computer without emotions and look at the situation, knowing all you've experienced. There is hope. Begin to name all the good things you have in your life: a place to live, someone who cares, food, a brain that works, a country where you have freedom of speech and you can worship as you wish.

In general I prefer not to listen to the news too often, but there are times that, in short doses, it helps me to appreciate my blessings. I may feel sorry for myself until I watch a story about earthquake survivors who have lost their entire

Step Three: Empower yourself.

families, homes, and jobs, and struggle just to remain alive and find food and water. Wow! I am blessed.

3. List your ideals and principals. What do you believe in? What gives you purpose and hope? Listen to your voice when you talk about a topic with your friends and family. What topics give you energy? What makes your voice rise and gets you excited? What makes you laugh? You might think you have no purpose now, but that's not true. Ask yourself, "What do I love to do? What has given me purpose and joy in the past?" Was it supporting and caring for your family, working at a meaningful job, helping others in some way?

All of these aspirations don't need to change after a trauma. Many people need your help. There are jobs available in the police force, the FBI, border patrol, firefighting, youth work, work with homeless people, home day care for both children and the elderly, and relief in the wake of disasters such as Hurricane Katrina (New Orleans), Superstorm Sandy (New York and New Jersey), and the flooding in Colorado. Get involved with working with refugees. If you're unable to get employment in these areas, volunteer your time and cooperate with others who believe in the same ideals that you do. We need you.

4. List your goals for the present and the future. What do you want your life to look like in five years? Ten years? What do you want to accomplish during that time? Who would you like to be in five years? Is there someone you admire? What is it you admire in her or him? Do you want to be more like this person? If so, select one area at a time you want to change in yourself, and begin. Again, focus on the things you have the power to change, not on factors out of your control. If you are married or have a long term partner, include her/him in this exercise. What are her/his goals? How can each of you compromise and make the goals comfortable for both of you?

5. List your priorities. Do you know what your priorities are? Many people think they do. But are they being honest? There is one sure way to find out. Check your actions. Are they congruent with what you say or think? For example, you may say your priority is family, yet you rarely have time to spend with your mate or children. You may say your priority is education, but you never check out what you can do to go back to school. You may say your priority is getting a job, but you don't apply because the position offered is not exactly what you want. Make sure your actions match your true priorities.

6. Organize your life. Create a consistent daily routine. Structure is essential. Make lists of what to do, what to buy, etc., and prioritize them. Researchers are finding that keeping lists can double or even triple your output a day. Plus they will decrease your stress level considerably and eliminate most crises in your life. Plan your week in advance. Place dates beside each item as to when you need to accomplish it. Include bills to pay and appointments to keep. Then go on to the next list. Before you go to bed, make a list of what you need to do the next day, step by step. Prioritize the steps

STEP THREE: EMPOWER YOURSELF.

by placing number 1 behind the most urgent one, number 2 behind the next, etc. The next day, strike out each item as you accomplish it. If life intervenes and you cannot get everything done by the date you set, place new dates on them. Reprioritize the list if need be. Be realistic. Life happens. There is only so much most of us can achieve in a single day or even a week.

7. Solve problems and make decisions. Here are some steps to follow when you have an important decision to make, such as finding a job or returning to school:

- Write down your problems in your notebook, leaving a few pages for each. Give yourself enough space to include what is going on in your life, what you think and feel about various issues.
- List as many possible solutions as you can think of. Leave some space after each solution. Be as creative as you can, even if you think the answer sounds silly or won't work (e.g., run away from home, live on a desert island, go out and fight). Some ideas will probably make you smile, but often they can be combined with other ideas or trigger thoughts of still more options that might work. Then do your research. Find out the facts. Call friends, businesses, or agencies, and look up data on the Internet. There may be more solutions than you knew existed.
- After each solution, list all the positives and negatives of that plan. If, for instance, you wish to buy stock in a company that you really believe will be profitable,

but you don't have the money and the interest rate on a loan is higher than the yield, you would probably eliminate this solution. Or if you consider family to be your priority and have been offered a job in Alaska and your family can't come with you, you might turn it down. On the other hand, if your family is willing to relocate or the company is willing to compromise and give you one week out of the month at home, you and your spouse or partner may agree to accept the job for a year to see how it works out.

- Go through each solution and place an x in front of each plan you know logically and intuitively won't work for you, and a check in front of each one that might work. Pick your battles. It's okay to say, "That solution may give me the outcome I desire, but the stress it would create in my life is more than I want or can handle at this point."
- Place a "1" after the solution you think will work best, a "2" after the second best, etc. See if you can combine some of the solutions.
- Some people have a difficult time coming up with answers for their problems. If that is you lie down somewhere comfortable, close your eyes, and take some deep breaths. Then imagine yourself in a safe place and ask your spiritual guide (some people think of God or Jesus), angel, or mentor to meet you there. Imagine the guide sitting next to you and talk to him or her about your problem. Let your guide direct you to what you need to do next or to an answer to help

Step Three: Empower yourself.

you. Make sure you listen instead of allowing your ego to take control of the situation.

8. Do things you succeed at to develop self-confidence.

- Write down all the things that keep you from becoming successful. List your feelings such as fear, shame, guilt, embarrassment, helplessness, and anger. Do you have unrealistic expectations? Or have you made poor choices in the past and are afraid you will make another decision that will have negative consequences?
- Sit comfortably in a chair, or lie down, and do some relaxation exercises such as breathing deeply, stretching, and clearing your mind. (Check Step Four for more details about relaxation). When you are relaxed, recall occasions when you felt capable and successful, creating a strong image in your mind of these incidents.
- As you maintain focus on your success for long periods of time, the wiring in your brain will actually change. Imagine, imagine, imagine success.

9. Now act. Do something you know you can successfully accomplish. Set yourself up for success by doing things you usually do well. If you know you can't hold a note, now is not the time to try singing an aria. Instead, if you are a good writer, why not write an article or a blog for a site you believe in? Several of the adults I saw wrote about their trauma and what they were doing to recover and then posted it on face book or a site that dealt with the topic. After a while you will be able to try new things. Progress usually takes place outside your comfort zone.

10. Change your body language. Your mind and body are very closely connected. Within a fraction of a second, your body will show what is going on in your mind, even though you are not aware of either the thought or the change in your body.

- First of all, become aware of what is happening in your body when you are under stress or you are in a difficult situation. Is your jaw tight or your fist clenched? Are your shoulders slumped and your head bowed? Are you frowning? Or do you glance away and avoid making eye contact with the person beside you? Other people pick up cues from your body language and react accordingly. If they perceive you to be a victim, they will treat you as a victim. If you come across as being angry and possibly violent, they tend to retreat and don't want to be near you. If they see you as powerful and assertive but not aggressive, they will recognize you as a leader and respect you.
- Become aware of your posture as you go about your day and meet challenges. Decide on what image you would like your bearing to portray.
- Practice in front of a mirror. Straighten your back and your shoulders, hold your head up high, swing your arms as you walk, and smile a genuine smile (one that affects your eyes as well as your mouth.)

STEP THREE: EMPOWER YOURSELF.

Look straight into someone's eyes, but not so long that you intimidate her or him.
- Next time you meet a challenge, like a job interview, check your body language immediately and change it if you need to, even though you may not feel like it. Act "as if." It will influence your mood and both your own and others' opinion of you. Role-play with a family member or friend before you go to a job interview.
- Clean up and dress up. In our culture, dressing in nice, clean clothes usually changes how we look at ourselves and how others see us. Feeling more confident automatically changes your body language. Your clothes and demeanor are particularly important when you are interviewing for a job. If you don't have the money to buy a suit (or whatever clothes are appropriate), visit thrift stores (they are called "once loved" clothing stores in New Zealand) where you can get great clothes for very little money.

11. Become future-directed. Take action. As much as possible, focus on the future, not on the past or on your current limitations. Maintain a positive expectation about the future. Although deciding what you want to do in the future is important, you must take action in order to make your life what you want it to be. Make plans for the present *and* the future. Then make them a reality. Now that you know what your goals are, write down a plan for how to get there. What do you need to do first? Next? If you are married or have a long-term partner, do this exercise together. Is she or he willing to help? In what way(s)?

12. Be realistic. When you act, you will run into obstacles you didn't expect. Whether we like it or not, the truth is that we are not in control of everything in our lives. The 12 step program has a prayer that the group repeats at every meeting. It is not religion-specific, but if you believe in a "higher power" than yourself, it can work for you. You may have heard it:

God grant me the Serenity to accept the things I cannot change, Courage to change the things I can, and Wisdom to know the difference.

Substitute your own word for God if you wish. It could be Creator, Higher Power, Allah, Jehovah, Life Force or whatever word you use to symbolize a power greater than yourself, in whom you trust. Write down the prayer and keep it where you can read it frequently. I keep a copy taped to my dining room hutch.

When you run into an obstacle, make a list of what you can and cannot control. You cannot control nature, such as the weather, disease, or natural disasters. You cannot control what other people think, say, or do. All you really can control is what **you** think, say, and do, and what meanings you attach to an event. Sometimes you can barely control those.

When you list the things you can control, see what you can change and work on those. But even those changes may not always alter the outcome, because you are not in control of how others respond or what happens in the larger world. I remember a time when I was asked to join an AIDS project

Step Three: Empower yourself.

in Africa. After hesitating, I finally came to the conclusion it was something I needed to do. The day after I said yes happened to be 9/11/01. In the aftermath of the terrorist attacks, all the money from overseas needed to move the project forward was frozen.

Any twelve-step program includes the adage, "Let go and let God." People often ask, "What does it mean to let go? Am I not supposed to try to change things?" No, that's not what is meant by that statement. To let go means you have done all the things you can to change what is happening in your life, but they haven't worked. You are becoming frustrated and trying harder and harder, but that approach still doesn't work. It's time to let go and turn the problem over to a greater power than yourself.

For example, imagine you have a sick child and you have taken him to the doctor and to a specialist. You've tried every drug and holistic medication available. You've prayed, begging continuously for the child's health to be restored, with no results. It is now time to admit you can't make him well, and that you must let go. It is time to allow and trust your higher power to take charge, regardless of what happens. Often you will come across information serendipitously that can help you.

Letting go is not an easy task, but it brings peace and acceptance into your life.

13. List what you have learned from your experience. How have you grown? Can you see a silver lining in the cloud? Did the trauma help you or save you somehow? Maybe you learned something about life or how to cope with it that will

always be of value to you. Maybe your beliefs and attitudes have changed. Maybe you have developed more empathy for others. Maybe you feel closer to your family than you ever did before the trauma. Instead of seeing only the negative consequences of the trauma, you can chose to look at positive ones as well.

When Jan, a long distance runner, was involved in a serious car accident she felt devastated. Although the emergency team saved her life, she took months to recover and was told she might never run again. But here is the silver lining: during the surgery after her injury, the doctors found that Jan had developed a serious heart problem. They immediately performed bypass surgery. The doctor told her that if she had not come to the attention of the medical staff, she might well have suffered a heart attack. Ultimately the injury may have saved her life.

STEP FOUR:
Learn to relax.

MANY OF YOUR PHYSICAL AND emotional symptoms of PTS decrease when you relax. Your blood pressure and pulse rate drop, your muscles loosen, and your anxiety lessens. If this does not occur, you may be someone for whom relaxation exercises increase anxiety. Usually this is not the case, but it does happen more frequently among PTSD sufferers. That's okay. For you, relaxing means you are not on alert, ready to act in case of an emergency. So there's a part of you that says, "It's dangerous to relax." Very understandable, since you encountered a dangerous occurrence that might have cost your life. If this is the case, skip the following suggestions for now. If relaxation exercises tend to increase your anxiety, simply exercising and flexing your muscles can help loosen them up and make you feel calm.

For most of you who can relax without negative effects, practice at least one technique that quickly relaxes your body and reduces your stress. The following exercises are easy and anyone can do them. But like so many things in life, it takes practice, practice, practice.

1. Do deep-breathing exercises. When you feel stressed, take time to breathe in and out, deeply and slowly, several times. Breathe in through your nose and out through your mouth, all the way, until you've emptied your lungs. Breathing in through your nose actually cools the amygdala (emotional brain) and reduces its reactivity. Put all your attention onto the rising and falling of your chest. Experience what the breath feels like in your body. Hear it going in and out. You will notice that when you breathe out fully, there is a moment that the muscles in your body relax naturally and completely.

2. Recognize what makes you relax. Is it an image, a sound, a smell, a feeling of an object or of your own body? The answer usually depends on the dominant sense (sight, hearing, smell, taste, or touch) that you use to communicate with the world. You may have two senses that both serve you well. Try using the different ones. Look at a picture, listen to your favorite music, smell something you like to smell, eat your favorite food or drink your favorite beverage, touch your favorite blanket. Lying on the fresh green grass and looking up at the sky works for me. After using each sense, check in with how your body feels.

3. Take a hot shower or bath. The heat of the water flowing over your body helps your muscles relax. Some people take a couple of showers a day, more to relax than to stay clean. My son used to stand in the shower for twenty minutes each evening so he could fall asleep more easily after a hard day at school.

Step Four: Learn to relax.

4. Remember a time (or times) in your life when you felt completely relaxed. You were able to relax because you felt safe. Write these memories down in your journal with as much detail as you can. For many of you, this may be a time spent outside, far away from other people. Others might recall sitting next to a stream, listening to a gurgling brook, or skipping rocks across a lake. Others will picture themselves indoors, maybe as a child at home with the family, or at Grandma's house, smelling her cooking and eating a piece of apple pie. Others may recall lying in bed, stroking a soft, fuzzy blanket, or playing with a cat or dog, or riding their horse. The place or time of your memory does not need to comply with other people's expectations. This is *your* journey.

Close your eyes. Now return to that place and time, imagining it in as much detail as possible. Imagine yourself in that environment, looking around in all directions. What do you see and hear? What do you smell? What do you feel or touch? How old were you when you were there? Allow yourself to fully relax in that place. Some people will fall asleep. That's okay. As a matter of fact, this is an excellent exercise to do if you have difficulty falling asleep.

Relaxing music helps. It is best to use one favorite piece over and over again each time you do these exercises, so that your mind can tie it to your feeling of relaxation.

5. Find a quiet spot where you will not be disturbed. Turn off your phone. If you're able, lie down and make sure you are comfortable. One of my clients used to go to the creek near her house and lie down in the long grass under a willow tree, far away from everyone. She would feel the earth and grass, see the mountains, smell the fresh air, and listen to the water gurgling in the stream.

6. Learn to move your mind away from everyday or worrisome thoughts.

- Pretend you are placing all your worries, one by one, onto the cloud floating by overhead, or into a container such as a box. Name the worries as you go. Close the container and lock it, then send it away on the clouds or down a stream or river. Watch the cloud or the container float farther and farther away and disappear.
- Another technique that works for some people is to play specific music (usually quiet, soft music) that takes their minds away and helps them relax. You need to experiment with the kind of music that works best for you.
- Some people hold an object that is symbolic of the place or feeling they wish to recall. It is comforting. One of my child clients found the perfect rock in the special creek near his house and placed it in his pocket where he could hold it tight and stop his tendency to fight with the other kids at school. Others carry a favorite soft piece of cloth or fur, a seashell, or other textured object they can touch. One person dabbed a little peppermint oil on her palm to remind her of her safe years in Idaho, growing up near her parents' peppermint fields. Any object can trigger relaxation if it has a quiet, safe memory attached to it.

STEP FOUR: LEARN TO RELAX.

7. Do a progressive relaxation exercise as an alternative to imagining a place. After you lie down and send away your worries, begin with your toes and move toward your head. Tense your toes, then tell yourself to relax them. Let them go limp. Then tense your foot and relax it, then your calf, your thigh, continuing up your body to your head. Breathe deeply in and out while you do this exercise.

8. Develop your own technique. The ones I've given you have helped many. However, each person is different. Feel free to create your own techniques if these don't work for you. For example, when one of my clients became anxious, she would stop whatever she was doing and do her own relaxation exercise. She would conjure up an image of mountains in her mind and take three deep breaths, and the stress would disappear like magic. When I asked her how she had started this practice, she said, "After the trauma, when I was stressed out and scared I remembered a verse I learned as a kid in Sunday school. It kept coming back to my mind. It's in Psalms: *I will lift up mine eyes unto the hills from whence cometh my help.* So I did that when things got tough. I imagined the mountains near our house in Montana, and then I would slowly breathe in that help, and I would know that I'd be okay." In other words, she created her own unique relaxation exercise that worked for her.

After you have done these exercises for a while—at least once daily for a couple of months—your body, mind, and emotions will trigger each other like Pavlov's dogs were triggered by the bell and the food. And so when you become anxious because of something that happened or something you thought, you will be able to take a few deep breaths, imagine your safe place and/or concentrate on your music, and immediately relax, feeling much less anxious. I can attest to you that relaxation and meditation work. It's how I was able to continue working for so many years with clients who dealt with PTSD.

STEP FIVE:
Become aware of yourself.

Self-awareness and self-knowledge are now frequently referred to as "mindfulness," though mindfulness has a broader definition that includes contemplation and meditation. (Meditation will be covered later in this book.) Mindfulness is a technique that can be used by virtually anyone to find balance in her or his life.

In this section I define mindfulness as being purposefully attentive to the present, using all your senses and noting your experiences and your responses to them. **To become self-aware and gain self-knowledge, you must practice staying in the here and now.**

It is common for people to be unaware of their bodily sensations, their feelings, and their thoughts. The more trauma you have experienced, the less likely you are to turn your focus inward. So why am I asking you to become aware of yourself? When you learn to recognize your thoughts, emotions, and physical sensations in the moment, you remain in the present and focus on them instead of on your triggers from the past, and therefore you are less reactive. You have more control in your life, which reduces stress and anxiety. You can see the bigger picture of what is important and what is not. This knowledge allows you to develop clearer thinking and concentration, and thus to change behaviors you don't like and that don't work for you anymore.

Awareness is the first step in changing your behavior. For example, maybe you have a habit of exploding when something stressful happens, or you distance yourself from the people you care about, or you go out and get drunk. Maybe you get angry and throw something, or you run away. But you don't know why you do these things, and often not even why you were stressed in the first place. The undesirable action just happens. Many people believe the behavior is automatic and they have no control over it. Actually this is false. Something is occurring in your mind, your feelings, and your body of which you are not aware.

If you are truly interested in changing the thoughts and behaviors that are not working for you and are causing you pain, if you want to become a more resilient person, you must become aware of what triggers these feelings. You must notice where the feelings lodge in your body, and what you are thinking when they occur. Until you can tap into them at one of these points inside or outside the body, you have little hope of understanding or changing the pattern. Recognizing how you react to a particular situation allows you to make a choice of what to do, instead of lashing out or running away automatically. **Having a choice helps you gain back your control.**

You are not a victim of your feelings, thoughts, and actions. Thoughts will come and go. Feelings will come and go. They are just that: thoughts and feelings. Don't give them so much credence or space in your life. They don't have that

Step Five: Become aware of yourself.

much power unless you allow them to take over your life. You have a choice as to how you will respond, act, and react. You do not need to say out loud everything you think. You do not need to act on every feeling you have. Again, you have a rational forebrain. If you count to ten before acting, or take yourself out of the situation immediately, you allow that part of your brain to engage. Then you can determine logically how you wish to act.

Just pay close attention to yourself.

Here's an easy check-in. Take a couple of minutes a day to get in touch with yourself. Take time alone in a quiet place so you don't get distracted by outside activity and noise. Whether you choose to stand, sit, or lie down, make sure you are comfortable.

1. Check your bodily sensations. Can you feel where your body touches the chair or ground? Are you feeling hot, cold, warm, comfortable? Are you relaxed or tense? If you are tense, in what areas of the body are you holding the tension and tightness? Your muscles will tell you. Are you shaking or perspiring? Is your heart racing? Do you have any pain? If so, where? Are you hungry? Sleepy? Tired? How is your breathing?

2. Check in with all your senses. What are you seeing right now? Describe it clearly. What are you hearing? Is someone playing music, or are the birds chirping? Is someone mowing the lawn? Can you hear cars? Listen to them carefully. What are you touching? Grass? Cloth? What does it feel like on your skin? Is there a taste you can detect in your mouth? Is there a smell you notice in your surroundings? Maybe it's the smell of flowers or newly mown grass, or a pungent odor, or the odor of sweat. The sense of smell triggers emotions more often than the other senses.

3. Check your feelings. People often say that when they close their eyes and focus on their hearts, they can get in touch more easily with their feelings. Ask yourself, "What am I feeling? Am I sad, happy, content, angry, anxious, afraid?" Some people will need to list various feelings and listen to their body after each one to see whether the feeling seems right.

4. Check your thoughts. What are the images and thoughts moving in and out of your conscious mind? Most of the time your feelings follow your thoughts. For example, you see a program on TV about hundreds of people losing jobs. You think, "Will I lose my job? My company isn't doing well financially." Then you begin to worry. Or you smell smoke in the air, which triggers thoughts of your house burning when you were young, making you feel sad and scared. Or you think of a sunny, relaxing day on the beach, and soon you feel happy, relaxed, and content. Some experts say that negative thinking is just a bad habit and can be changed. (For more about thoughts and how to alter them, see Step Seven)

5. Stay in the here and now. Take on a job or project where your mind cannot wander. Bruce, a former police officer had constant trauma memories of his years in the LAPD. I asked him how he had survived. He said, "I took a job as

Step Five: Become aware of yourself.

a bulldozer operator for a lumber company. It forced me to stay right there. My mind couldn't wander, or else I would have been in big trouble." (Not that I suggest getting a job as dangerous as this. There are other ways to stay in the here and now.) Another woman, a rape survivor became a wildlife photographer. She immersed herself in getting the "perfect photo." Not only did she have to remain in the present to do so, but she had a lot of fun. Doing something creative that also stretches your mind is indeed one way to remain excited, immersed and happy. Researchers say it's one of the best ways to break depression.

6. Talk to yourself. I imagine you learned at a young age that talking to yourself was a sign of being "weird" or "crazy." Other kids made fun of you. So you learned to shut down the voices in your mind, thus losing the self-awareness you once had. I suggest that you talk to yourself. But this time, you can do it internally or, if you need to speak out loud, do it when you are alone. Pretend you are two different people, and argue with yourself about an issue. Actually, although we are not "split," we have several different parts of ourselves we can identify. Often they can be identified as being different ages or having different issues. There are various voices inside us most of the time. When we have a decision to make, two or more sides of ourselves can emerge and discuss or argue with each other. Listen to these voices inside you, or speak out loud. Become aware of the process.

Some of you may have heard of a technique called Gestalt Therapy. In very basic terms, it entails talking to yourself, and is a very powerful way of getting in touch with your inner selves. Imagine the part of you, or the organ that is giving you trouble, or the person with whom you are having difficulty, sitting on the chair across from you. (If that's difficult for you to imagine, place an object on the chair, such as a pillow, that symbolizes the other person or part of yourself.) Then talk to that person or part of yourself as though he/she/it were present right now. Ask him/her/it any questions you wish and write down the answers that first come into your mind. For example, "Who are you? What do you look like? What are you feeling right now? What are you thinking? What is making you so sad or angry?" When you have finished asking questions of these pretend other persons, and having them answer your questions, ask yourself, "What do I want or need to say to that person or part of me?" Then tell that part or person what you would like to say.

If you can't get answers to all the questions mentioned in this section, don't be discouraged. Most people have to learn how to become aware of themselves and must practice frequently.

As an example, I worked with an Iraq veteran committed to change. Each time he came to my office, he would march in, looking much like the officer he had been in the army. He looked in control. One time he sat down and told me that he had just heard of a close friend who had died in battle. He showed little emotion.

I asked him, "What are you feeling as you tell me this?"

He looked puzzled and shook his head. "I don't know. I don't feel anything. Why are you asking?"

"Well, you just told me that a close friend of yours from your unit died in battle. How does that affect you?"

Step Five: Become aware of yourself.

He swallowed hard. "Oh, okay. I guess I'm sad."

"Where in your body are you feeling it?"

He shrugged and tried to change the subject.

"Emotions are very powerful," I said. "I know that part of you doesn't want to get in touch with them, but the PTSD symptoms won't go away if you don't."

He grunted.

"Picture your body. How do you see yourself?"

He suddenly laughed. "I have steam coming out of my nostrils. I want to kill the men who killed him. I'm very angry."

"What are you thinking right now?"

"Those bastards." And on and on.

We placed the "pretend steaming" person on a chair and dialogued with him. You can do this in a journal as well. Write out both sides of the conversation, like a dialogue in a play.

You don't have to start immediately by becoming aware of difficult feelings. Instead, start with an easy situation. When you go to a restaurant, look around the room and ask yourself which booth would make you feel most relaxed. Test it out. Then try another one. Feel what feels wrong or good in your body. Do the same when you check out the menu.

The sensations in your body will help you make decisions. Some people think that your body or intuition will always lead you right. Often your intuition does help guide you, but I haven't found that it is right every time. Maybe that means most of us, including me, aren't good enough at listening to our bodies to get it right. I don't know.

I suggest that, before you make any important decision in your life, you use a healthy dose of brain power and logic as well. Sometimes your body hums with your desires instead of what is good for you. Learn as much as you can about a subject first. Check your priorities. Write down the positives and negatives of each decision. Check Step Three for exercises on decision making and problem solving. Then ask your body what it's trying to tell you.

My husband and I had some money to invest, and we began to explore different options. Friends we trusted asked us to join them in a "sure" investment deal. That should have been our first warning. It was an innovative idea, but there was little information about the area available for us to check. So we decided to ask our intuition about what was best. The adventure sounded right for us at the time, and the possibilities seemed limitless. We jumped without looking squarely at the risk. In the long run we lost our investment. Intuition was not enough.

If you find something you wish to invest in—time, energy, or money—do it knowing clearly what your potential positive outcomes and risks might be. Of course, there are no sure outcomes, but you can mitigate risks by playing it smart.

7. Change your behaviors. When you are fully aware of your physical sensations, your feelings, and your thoughts, it is time to change your behavior to what you wish it to be. Start by running a film in your mind that shows you acting appropriately when something sets you off. Replay this image many times a day. Don't forget that you may still make mistakes when an actual event happens that triggers your

Step Five: Become aware of yourself.

habitual response, even when you know better. Don't be too hard on yourself. You are human. You don't go from grade three to grade eight in one jump. It's all about learning and practicing.

STEP SIX:

CHECK WITH A DOCTOR TO SEE WHETHER MEDICATIONS CAN HELP.

IN MOST CASES WHERE SYMPTOMS are severe, I believe in working on all aspects of a problem at once— emotional, mental, spiritual, and physical—in order to alleviate the severity of symptoms, so people can return to some degree of functioning. If you need relief immediately, it is clear from research that a combination of psychotherapy and medication works more rapidly and effectively than either approach alone. There are many medications that can help you cope with PTS and PTSD. New ones are constantly being discovered. If you are not on any medication at present but you have severe symptoms of PTS, consult your doctor or a psychiatrist. Medications along with therapy can help you stabilize.

Discuss the possibility of using medications with your doctor and your counselor. You will want to be cautious about the length of time you are on medications, but never go off them without consulting your doctor. As a word of warning, it is always advisable to check out any medication for negative side effects that can create more problems than the original symptoms.

Step Six: Check with a doctor to see whether medications can help.

This section will be fairly brief because I am not a medical doctor and do not pretend to know what medications you need. I merely list a few options that your doctor may prescribe according to your symptoms.

If you are depressed, doctors most often order the latest antidepressants, selective serotonin reuptake inhibitors (SSRI's), such as Prozac, Zoloft, and Lexapro. Sometimes, depending on your situation, they will prescribe older medications called tricyclics, such as Imipramine. Normally it takes about three weeks for antidepressants to work effectively. Sometimes you may take a drug that doesn't seem to work, and your doctor may need to switch to another one before you find the right one. Also, don't forget that if you decide to discontinue an antidepressant, you can't suddenly stop your medication. If you do, you may become even more depressed. You must reduce the dosage slowly, under the advice of a physician.

For treatment resistant depression ask your doctor about ketamine. Esketamine can be transfused intravenously with rapid relief (usually in less than a day). It has been found to be very effective for many who can get no or little relief from antidepressants.

If you suffer from nightmares, Minipress (generic name: Prazosin), a blood pressure medication, is one of the drugs frequently prescribed. Prazosin makes people less sensitive to adrenalin and reduces nightmares. You may also be given beta blockers. These are heart medications that reduce hyperarousal and block the effects of adrenalin. Anti-anxiety medication, such as Ativan, Klonopin , and Xanax, work for severe anxiety, but are used with caution because they are addicting.

An antibiotic, D-cycloserine, is now used to treat fears. It enhances fear extinction, especially when used with Prolonged Exposure Therapy (PET). (I will discuss PET in Step Eleven.) If you have problems sleeping, there are several drugs your physician can prescribe. Newer drugs such as Ambien usually do not leave you feeling "hung over" in the morning. For people with co-occurring disorders such as bipolar disorder, mood stabilizers can help. For those who have been physically injured and find themselves in intense pain a great deal of the time, pain killers such as oxycoton or hydrocodone are frequently prescribed. These drugs are narcotics and are addicting.

Different medications work more effectively for some people than others. It may be necessary to try several drugs before your doctor finds the right combination that works for you. Hang in there and don't give up. For an extra fee, not usually covered by your health insurance, you can now be tested for genetically optimal medications.

There are many drugs for particular symptoms, but so far, none that will modify or erase distressing memories. With the rapid increase of research being conducted on the brain and memory at present, scientists are now on the verge of discovering a solution. The age of memory treatment is here.

Although still not approved for PTSD, two promising drugs that are currently undergoing research may be of interest to you. As mentioned earlier, during a freeze, fight, or flight response, adrenaline sears vivid emotional memories of trauma into the brain with the help of the amygdala. Researchers have recently discovered that a low dose of Proprananol, a blood pressure medication and beta

Step Six: Check with a Doctor to See Whether Medications Can Help.

blocker, reduces activity in the amygdala and subdues the freeze, fight, or flight response. Users of Proprananol do not forget the memory, but are actively able to redesign and reconsolidate it. The drug strips away the terror of the trauma while leaving the facts behind, and has been found to be most useful shortly after the trauma has occurred. A McGill University research group collaborating with Harvard psychiatrist Roger Pitman found that after several treatments with Proprananol, PTSD symptoms declined by half and stayed that way even after six months.

At present the U.S. Army has designated $6.7 million to research drugs that go beyond Proprananol. At present psychedelics such as psilocybin, and LSD are again being researched to reduce psychological distress with favorable results. Studies are also being conducted with 3-4 methylenedioxy-methamphetaminetames (MDMA), the active ingredient of the street drug Ecstasy. As does Proprananol, MDMA tames the brain's fear center, the amygdala, allowing PTSD survivors to confront bad memories as necessary, during a session with a psychotherapist, without a great deal of fear. They still feel some fear, but trust themselves to go past it. The drugs act similarly to anti-anxiety medications, but without the sedative effects. The patient is free of pain. Michael Mithoefer, a psychiatrist in South Carolina, has found that seventeen out of twenty subjects in his small pilot study no longer met the criteria for PTSD after two or three sessions with MDMA and prolonged exposure therapy. The drug is still experimental, and possible side effects have not yet been established.

As research continues into memory, neurobiologists have found that certain chemicals in the memory process, when given in high doses, can literally blank out specific memories in animals as the memories are being recalled. They have also discovered ways of eliminating whole categories of memories. Their approval for use in humans is probably still years away.

For most people, this selective memory erasure sounds terrifying. What if the medication doesn't work as scientists think it will, and instead wipes out *all* memories? Yet in spite of the risks, according to researchers, there are people "standing in line" who wish to be research subjects. Many of them are rape survivors.

At present, a third of all PTSD survivors do not recover completely, but the future is promising for severely traumatized persons.

STEP SEVEN:

Change your thinking.

Though separating the emotions, mind, body, and spirit is not possible in reality, I have done so for the purpose of listing steps as logically as possible. So bear with me if some of the next sections overlap somewhat.

It is now believed that the following is the process to change old habits:

Self-awareness—>change old thoughts—>this changes feelings—> now change your behavior—>new neural pathways are formed. Repeat this new pattern often and it strengthens the pathways in the brain until the new change becomes reflexive (a habit).

Along with Step Eleven, where I describe Prolonged Exposure Therapy (PET), Step Seven is known to be the most effective way to help you recover from severe stress after a trauma. Research shows that these two steps used together are up to 95% effective in treating PTS. But these are not easy steps to do, and many people stop practicing them before they see lasting results. So stick with them. I am confident that if you change your thinking and then change your behavior, you will change your life.

When I speak of the mind, I am talking both of that which is conscious and known to you and that which is unconscious and unknown to you. Except for reflexes (ingrained habits) and instincts, such as the freeze, fight, or flight survival response that literally can save your life, most psychologists and scientists now believe that your unconscious and/or conscious thoughts actually occur just prior to your emotions, not the other way around. Try it for yourself. Think of a time when you did something you loved to do. How do you feel? Now think of a difficult time in your life. How do you feel? The thought comes first, then comes the emotion.

With practice you can observe your thoughts and learn to change them, thereby changing your emotions. When you modify your thoughts about a situation, you alter your stress level and your depression. Negative thinking increases your stress and depression; positive thinking decreases it.

Does thinking about something actually attract to you what you want or don't want, as some people claim? I really don't know. But I do know from experience that thoughts change our happiness factor and our resilience. They change our outlook on life. They make us aware of our options. Even so, it is still up to us to make decisions and take actions.

Unconscious, implicit beliefs lead to thoughts, then to emotions, and then to actions. Without changing your actions, your dreams will not become reality. One of my clients, who felt very lost when he stopped drinking and doing drugs after years of childhood abuse, came up with a plan for a business. He was excited about what he was going to

Step Seven: Change your thinking.

do and thought about it constantly. But he never took any action. I imagine you know how the story ended.

Though negative thinking is partly genetic, you have programmed negative thoughts about yourself into your mind over many years. (If you didn't, psychologists would probably call you a narcissist.) Maybe people in your past reminded you, or at least implied, that you were "stupid" or that you were a "failure," and you have incorporated those voices into your thinking. Scientists now believe that about 90% of your thoughts come from your past experiences and automatically run through your mind daily without you being aware of them.

I have mentioned the word "perception" in Part 1. Your perception of yourself, of others, and of events is the key to your success and happiness. What is your perception of yourself? Those programmed voices from the past determine how you see yourself, often on an unconscious level. Occasionally your inner voices tell you that you are so terrific, you don't need to change. That is rare. Usually they say phrases like, "I can't do it," "I'm bad," "I have no control," "Terrible things can happen to me and I won't see them coming," or "I have to be alert all the time to be prepared." Interestingly, research indicates that chronic anxiety is more common among people whose family history fosters the perception that aversive events are unpredictable and uncontrollable.

A highly effective form of treatment for reducing and managing PTS is called Cognitive Therapy. Briefly, Cognitive Therapy teaches you how to change your perception and your thoughts in order to control anxiety and depression. Treatment gains have been shown to be long-lasting. As you change your thinking new pathways are forged in the brain and the more you reinforce these pathways with your new thinking, the more they become a habit and automatic. Your old thoughts from childhood are like a rut in a road. The more you use it the deeper it gets. Somewhere you realize that rut isn't working and you must create a new path.

Many people think they have no control over their thoughts. Wrong. Your mind is malleable, and what you think is knowable and therefore largely in your control. That's comforting. Believing you have no control in your life causes much more stress. You must become aware of your thoughts or you can't change them. For example, you may feel sadness, guilt, and maybe anger. However, you are not aware of what you were thinking. All you understand is the emotion, and sometimes not even that. But you can learn. You are no longer in a traumatic situation, and it's time to move on, to gain some control over your emotions and thoughts so you can live a normal life.

A word of caution: If you are still in a traumatic situation such as an abusive relationship, dangerous city streets, or war, I caution you to please first practice Step 3 to make you feel strong enough to ask for help and find a way out.

HOW CAN YOU CHANGE YOUR THOUGHTS?

Thoughts are so automatic that they run like a continuous CD. When I asked my clients what they were thinking just prior to the flashback, fear, or anger, the majority did not know. Most of them looked puzzled and said, "I'm not thinking anything. It just happens. My anger is just suddenly there."

Step Seven: Change your thinking.

If you aren't aware of what you are thinking, you are not alone. Most people don't know what their unconscious thoughts are, and they frequently have no idea what to do about their feelings. Many people don't even know what they are feeling. Someone says to you, "You look angry. What's going on?" and you say, "What are you talking about? I'm not angry." The truth is that you were thinking about something that triggered the anger, but both the thought and the feeling were unconscious.

I hate to admit that I used to be a perfectionist. Well, according to some people who know me, I still am— just a bit, of course. When I first decided to change my thinking, I began to listen to the messages my mind was giving me. After a while, I realized that several times a day, someone inside my mind kept saying, "It doesn't matter how hard you try, you'll never do it well enough." The voice didn't say, "You're a terrible, no-good louse," but that regardless of what I did, I'd never figure out how to get it right, even though I had no way of knowing what the word *right* meant. I knew one thing. How could I possibly succeed if that's what I was telling myself over and over again? Wow! Now I had a choice.

It became a challenge for me to become aware of what I was thinking. So I did what I thought of as a research experiment. After I felt any emotion, negative or positive, I stopped and asked myself, "What am I thinking?" After a while, that little voice inside began to answer. When I experienced joy, the inner voice spoke of positive things I had accomplished, or of happy memories from my past, or of creative and exciting things I had planned for in the future. It talked to me of the people and places I loved. When I was sad, fearful, or angry, it spoke of something negative, like a loss, a difficult memory, or a frightening event that had happened or might happen in the future. Thus I felt anxious and depressed.

Where do these voices come from? Usually they come from the past, from family, teachers, friends, work, the culture at large. Where had I learned to believe that I wasn't good enough? My parents and many of the people around me were perfectionists. Without meaning to, they gave me the impression I had to be perfect, whatever that meant. However, deep inside I knew I could never achieve that perfection.

One of my clients said she remembered the exact day as a child when she finally accepted her parents' messages that she was an evil child. She spent time and a lot of energy changing those messages, and is now a physicist at a national research laboratory.

Figuring out where the messages came from is enlightening, but more important is to understand that your mind has accepted those messages and is feeding them back to you daily, at numerous times and in numerous ways. You are not different or weak for having these thoughts. Everyone has them.

On the other hand, some realistic expectations and self-judgment are positive. If a student gets an F on her paper and the professor, teacher, or parent gives her a gold star or other reward, she probably won't try to improve. But if the teacher says, "You are intelligent, but you really don't know the subject well enough to pass this course and you'll need to

Step Seven: Change your thinking.

get a tutor to catch up," the student will have higher expectations of herself and probably achieve more in life.

Now that the data about our youngest generation—often called the "self-esteem generation"— is coming in, we are finding that many of those kids have little motivation to change, strive to do better, work hard, or even compete with themselves or others. Accustomed to receiving praise for merely existing, they have nothing to achieve. Some think they are owed rewards and that everything should be given to them. They believe they can do whatever they feel like and they'll still "pass the grade" without having to work for it. Then when they get out into the real world, they have a tough time adjusting to the expectations of an employer, a spouse, and even society.

If you are honest and realistic with yourself, you can learn a great deal from adversity. You can grow stronger. You can handle more setbacks and cope better with life's ups and downs.

1. Become aware of your thoughts:

- **Journal in a free-flowing way, without thinking about what you are writing.** Then read it back to yourself, out loud. Several times a day, ask yourself what you are thinking at that moment. A good time to practice this is when you have reacted to a problem in a way you didn't consciously want to and have no idea why you did so, or when you experience any strong feeling. Ask yourself, "What am I thinking?" Don't just say, "I don't know." Tell your mind it has permission to answer without being judged for the answer.

- **Pretend you are talking to your mind.** Imagine your mind in any way that comes to you. A lot of people envision their mind as another person who has the answers, a mentor, or a wise guide to whom they can ask a question. Then talk to it, ask it questions, and listen to its answers. Crazy? Maybe, but your mind is magnificent and powerful, and holds the answers inside. This technique has worked for many people in my practice.
- **Use free association.** Freud discovered this technique many years ago, and it still works well. In free association, you say a word or think of an incident, and whatever image first comes into your mind is what the unconscious mind is associating with that word or incident. Make a list of at least four associations. For example: War—gunpowder—explosions—screams—death. Free association may help you with dreams or to dig down to what is really bothering you.
- **Listen to your body.** Some people wonder how to know for sure that they have received the right answer when using these techniques. You won't always know, but most of the time, the words or images that surface fit the situation. Your mind and body are so closely related that the body will respond almost instantaneously to your thoughts. Either it will tense up and your heart will start racing, or it will relax and slow down. Some people say, "It just feels right." My husband knew when he was on the right track when tears

Step Seven: Change your thinking.

came to his eyes. If you are not aware of what you are thinking or feeling, pay attention to your body, which will respond moments after your thoughts.

Notice when and where your muscles tense. Are you gritting your teeth? Are you tapping your foot? Ask yourself, "Why am I tapping my foot? What am I feeling?" You may find that usually you tap your foot when you are anxious, grit your teeth when you are angry, and smile when you are happy. Then ask yourself, "What was I thinking that brought on that reflex?"

2. Change your thoughts and reprogram your brain. Change your thoughts, change your feelings. Changing your thinking has been found to be as useful for treating depression as chemical antidepressants, although it takes longer to retrain your brain than to take a medication. However, as long as you practice this step, the effect remains. Your mind is literal, and it will believe what you tell it, if the thought is repeated often enough. When you change your thinking about an event or trauma, your perception of it also changes. Have you ever heard the phrase, "Well, it all depends on how you look at it." That's what I mean. **Here are several ways to change your thinking:**

- **Educate yourself about PTS and PTSD** so that you know the facts, not the myths and rumors. Read this book and any other reliable resource.
- **Read positive literature.** Depending on your preference, read inspirational stories and positive self-help

books (*Feeling Good* by David Burns is a classic in the field—see the Suggested Readings page), or spiritual literature, such as the Bible, other religious books, or spiritual meditations. Make sure the books you choose induce a hopeful feeling inside you and don't increase your fears, depression, and hopelessness. (No help needed in that department. You are already doing that all by yourself.)

- **Make positive statements or affirmations.** Once you become aware of your thoughts, it is time to do something about them. As I said earlier, the mind is malleable and literal, and it will believe what it is told over and over again. That's how a politician can convince you of what he wants you to believe. Just repeat the lie or half truth (or whatever you prefer to call it) often enough, in an authoritative way and your mind says, "Yes." Try it. Some books tell you to merely rephrase the thought into the opposite positive response and repeat it over and over. Each time you hear yourself saying something negative to others or to yourself, turn it around. For example, if you hear yourself saying or thinking, "I am stupid and will never master these techniques," switch to "I choose to change my thoughts. I am wise, and my mind learns easily."

Dr. Mark William Cochran, a chiropractor, energy worker and speaker, says in his book *Oby's Wisdom: A Caveman's Simple Guide to Holistic Health and Wellness,* "Know that affirmations are not an accurate description of what is going on for you now.

Step Seven: Change your thinking.

It is not the reality you desire. Your affirmations are statements to affirm the truth that you have decided to create for yourself."

- **Change your story.** What is the internal story you have created about yourself? About having PTS or PTSD? Dr. Cochran frequently speaks about how he dealt with a severe arthritic condition he developed while in the Marines, and how he regained his health to the point that he was able to run a marathon. He says that the single biggest factor in recovering his health was changing his story about himself.

  For years he held the identity of a guy with a debilitating and crippling disease, even though he was doing everything he could to **fight** the disease. Ultimately he realized that his perspective was keeping him locked into the disease. **He shifted his focus from fighting to thriving.** Rather than let himself be driven by the disease, he recognized that he had an amazing power within himself to heal. We all do. His thoughts and actions shifted, and today he does everything he can to allow his internal healing wisdom to work to its maximum potential.

- **Choose your focus.** Where is your focus? Focus on greatness, not on your limiting beliefs. When negative thoughts occur, acknowledge them and then tell your mind that you will not focus on them. Focus on aliveness, energy, and love, and be grateful for your life.

  A few years ago, my husband, whom I loved *so* very much, lay on his death bed. As I sat beside him in his hospice bed, I checked in on my thoughts several times a day. I would tell myself, "Anna, You are so very scared and sad but you have a choice as to what you focus on in your thoughts at this moment. You have a choice as to how you will respond to this situation." Sometimes I could refocus on the present or I could call a friend for support. Often times, however, I remained in my deep sense of impending loss. But at least I knew I could change my thinking, even though it might have been only for a moment.

- **Talk to yourself.** As you become more aware of negative thoughts and beliefs that are not working for you, talk to yourself. Usually the thoughts and beliefs come from the past and are not really true, so convince your mind that these thoughts have little to do with you now. Use words such as, "That really isn't true. I am a capable person. Just because I blew it this time doesn't mean much. I have been successful in many ways in my life." Then name the times you've been successful.

- **Watch a positive, inspirational, or funny movie or listen to music that calms you.** Nature sounds, meditation CDs, guitar music, and other soft music usually calm your mind. Very loud music, such as hard rock, can be jarring and make you feel more depressed. Don't see movies or play songs that you know tend to make you feel depressed or agitated. For each individual, this will be different. For example, I go into an immediate funk listening to country

Step Seven: Change your thinking.

music songs about all the spurned lovers who would rather die than go on without their sweetheart.
- **Use a mantra.** Another way to change your thoughts is to repeat a calming word or phrase over and over to yourself. Find a positive phrase that calms and comforts you such as, "Love will overcome." Some people use vocalizations such as "Ohm." Some people in twelve-step programs repeat the Serenity Prayer many times a day (see Step Ten). This prayer is not religion-specific. Some people use verses from their favorite religious text that reassure them and bolster their beliefs.

    Another classic book, *The Power of Positive Thinking* by Norman Vincent Peale, is a resource in which several of my Christian clients have found mantras. In it, Peale suggests repeating portions of positive Bible verses. Two verses he mentions are, "I can do all things through Christ who strengthens me," and "If you have faith as small as a mustard seed, you can move mountains."
- **Accept both the negative and the positive. This world is a place of duality.** We live with constant unconscious tensions between opposites. They are undeniable and are permanent experiences in our lives (success, failure; love, rejection; joy, sadness; good, bad). Denying them and constantly trying to find a way to get rid of the "bad" feelings can be expensive and take most of our time and energy. There's a good reason the brain immediately tries to find a solution to this dilemma. The biological reason your mind automatically tries to

banish the dark side is to feel good and thus survive. If you accept both sides as neither good or bad, just there, you will suddenly see that the tension between opposites is the normal flow like a river winding back and forth through life. For more information read the book *Unflappable: Six Steps to Staying Happy, Centered, and Peaceful No Matter What* by Ragini Elizabeth Michaels.

- **Reframe your thoughts.** Change the meaning that an event or experience holds for you. Look at a situation from a different angle. You don't need to deny reality, but you do have a choice as to where you want your mind to spend most of its time. You can shine a flashlight on the problem or the solution, on the positive or the negative side of the issue. The positive is no less true than the negative, just located at the other end of the spectrum called life. It must, however, ring true, at least to some extent.

  People have the option to view negative experiences as opportunities to learn from and become better people. They might say, "This trauma has given me an opportunity to understand how other people feel in similar situations." They can ask themselves, "What have I learned from this? How can I gain strength from adversity? How can I remain optimistic and hopeful in this situation?" They can choose to focus on the silver lining in the cloud, rather than on the darkness. As they reframe their thoughts, they grow and become stronger. **This means you are becoming more resilient.**

3. **Practice Rational Emotive Behavior Therapy.** For many people, affirmations only feel like lies and veer too far from their beliefs to accept. They think, "This is not true. I'm not safe. Anything could happen at any time. I have no control. I am just lying to myself when I come up with these unrealistic, positive ways of thinking about the trauma and myself." If this is how you feel, Rational Emotional Behavior Therapy might be for you.

In 1955 Dr. Albert Ellis developed a technique called Rational Emotive Behavior Therapy (REBT) as a realistic and more "honest" way to work with thoughts. This technique will help you change your thinking slowly and rationally, so that you can believe what you are saying to yourself. The technique is quite simple. All you will need is a sheet of paper and a pen:

- **Divide your paper into three columns.**
- **After a stressful incident, monitor your thoughts and feelings** This takes practice, but need take only a few minutes a day. What are your current beliefs? The trauma may well have changed them. Perhaps you used to believe you were safe, that you could trust people, and that you were in control of your life, but not anymore. If you are not aware of your thoughts, stop yourself each time you experience a strong feeling. If anger is your main issue, notice the anger and stop. Ask yourself, "What am I thinking?" Or "What am I angry about?" Allow an answer to come to you. Accept whatever first enters your mind. Usually it is correct. For example, a common

thought for people with PTS is, "I have no control. Things will never change. I can't handle this anymore." Other common thoughts are "Everything is going to hell. Nobody loves me. The world is a terrible place." Or, "I'll never get a job. I might as well give up." Then look at what triggered the thought. It can be something very small, such as your mate frowning at you, or your son rebelling against you.

- **Once you are aware of your physical sensations, your automatic beliefs and thoughts, and your feelings, write them down in the first column.** Usually the negative thoughts are "always" and "never" thoughts. "This will never change." Or you might be creating catastrophes in your mind such as "The world is coming to an end.", or maybe you are over-generalizing, thinking that "everyone" is not to be trusted, instead of just the one person who hurt you. Some people call this "stinking thinking."

  When you do this exercise, also notice your happy and contented thoughts. "I love sitting here looking out at the mountains with no danger nearby." Or, "It's so nice to connect with my son." Or, "Gosh that spaghetti tastes good." This will give you an idea of what makes you happy.

- **Now ask yourself, "How true are my negative thoughts?" Use the second column to write down what is logically true.** Whenever you find yourself saying or thinking words such as "always" and "never," check yourself. Is that really true? Is it true that things will never change? Are you sure? How do you know?

Step Seven: Change your thinking.

Think of times things have changed for you. Maybe you say to yourself, "I can't handle it anymore. I'm too weak." In reality, you've handled many situations until now and survived. Sure, all humans have weaknesses, but what are the strengths you have that have helped you survive life thus far? What can you do to get help? Name specific strengths and instances when you have come through a stressful situation. Remember what you did and what worked for you.

- **Now reframe your thoughts so they make sense to you.** In the third column, rewrite what is really true. Say, "My thoughts at the time were not true, but this is what is really true. There are times I feel weak, like right now, but there have been many times when I've been strong." List a few past incidents to remind you.
- **Practice. Practice. Practice.** You may be getting tired of this word, but it's the best way to continue your recovery and make it long-lasting. Soon you'll be able to complete the exercise in your mind without writing it down, though it is still good to write it down so you can review it whenever you need to.
- **Now determine the behavior you wish to change and how you wish to go about it.** Check Step Eight for ideas on how to do this.
- **Take action.**

STEP EIGHT:
CHANGE UNWANTED BEHAVIORS

I ADDRESS BEHAVIORS BEFORE I LOOK at how to work with feelings because usually behaviors are less difficult for people to deal with than their emotions.

Change is difficult for humans. We gravitate toward what is familiar and feels safe. That's the way our brain works, and old habits die slowly. Just thinking differently and feeling differently about something is great, but in order to be in control of your life again, you must change your actions as well. We are not in control of many things outside ourselves, but most of the time we are in control of our own behaviors (actions and reactions). Did you know that long-lasting change is most likely to occur during a crisis like the one you may be undergoing at present? People will do almost anything to get rid of physical and/or emotional pain. But depending on people's tolerance levels, it may take extraordinary pain and discomfort to motivate them to grow and change. Growth usually takes place outside our comfort zone.

You may have heard the saying, "The pain must outweigh the gain you receive from a negative behavior." I don't believe it is necessary to "hit bottom" before you change, but I do know that pain is one of the greatest motivators in

Step Eight: Change unwanted behaviors

the world. On the other hand, sometimes the motivator can be something positive, such as love, money, relationships, or happiness.

Always, the motivation to change a behavior starts with a strong feeling. Whenever you react or act in response to a strong feeling, there will be consequences, either positive or negative. When you are hungry, you eat. When you are lonely, you visit a friend. When you are in love, you struggle to be with the person you love. When you believe someone wants to harm you or someone you love, you run or fight. When you lose your job and your spouse or partner threatens to leave, you stop drinking. First the feeling, then the action.

Here are some ideas to help you change your behavior:

1. Make a list of behaviors you would like to change. Why do you wish to change them? What negative consequences are you experiencing because of these behaviors? Write the consequences below each behavior, so that you can read them several times when you are tempted to forget about the changes you wish to make.

2. Prioritize the list. What behavior is causing you the most pain? Are you eating too much or drinking too much or doing drugs, and therefore you have lost your job and/or your family? Are you violent, or staying in a violent relationship? Write these behaviors in order of the pain they cause you.

3. Ask yourself, what would create the greatest gain in your life if you changed that behavior? What is most important to you? Your family? A job? Sometimes the greatest pain and the greatest gain come from the same behavior (but not always).

4. Intentionally choose one behavior on the list you wish to change immediately. I imagine you want to change all of them at once, but that would be setting yourself up for failure. Take one behavior at a time. It may not be the hardest behavior to change. Sometimes it is better to choose an easier, less consequential one to begin with, so that you can experience a quick success to boost your confidence.

5. Identify the feeling that best motivates you to change a specific behavior. Allow yourself to feel that feeling completely (e.g., fear of losing your partner and kids). Bring to mind various events that trigger that feeling. Then cultivate the ability to remember and shift into that state at will. This will motivate you to continue on your new path. For example, one of my clients found herself eating more and more and gaining weight because of her frustration at not finding a job. Then she met a friend she had not seen for some time who had gained a lot more weight than she had. Her friend had a great deal of difficulty getting up the stairs and even walking to her car. As a nurse, my client had thrived on being healthy and active. The terror of losing the ability to move at will motivated her to exercise to relieve stress, instead of eating. Every time she wanted to eat when stressed, she held the image of her friend in her mind and felt the fear of becoming helpless. When she did this, the need to overeat would vanish for the time being.

STEP EIGHT: CHANGE UNWANTED BEHAVIORS

Also remember occasions when you distinctly experienced the feelings you want to feel, such as pride, joy, and relaxation. Positive feelings are as effective as negative ones for motivating behavioral changes. Practice shifting into good feelings, like the nurse who wanted to stop overeating. She told me how proud she felt of herself when she said no to a donut her husband had offered her. That feeling of pride was almost as effective in motivating her to eat properly as was her fear of becoming disabled.

6. Look at your behavior and ask yourself how you are benefitting from it. What have you gained from continuing the behavior that outweighs the pain it causes? Maybe you get more attention. Maybe your addiction has eased your physical and emotional pain, at least for short periods, so you feel you can continue living. (Because drugs stimulate the pleasure center in your brain and increase the dopamine level, sobriety is even harder to maintain than other behavior changes.) Maybe lashing out releases your anger and makes you feel more powerful again.

7. Are you motivated enough to actually carry out long-term behavioral changes?

- What will happen if you continue as you have been? Might your loved one leave?
- How would you feel if that happened? Do you really, really want him or her to stay?
- What would have to happen to make life so painful that you would change your behavior to avoid it?

What reward would make the change worthwhile? Is there a different, more positive behavior that will still give you the rewards you crave?

8. Consider not only this week, but the years to come. Now set up a plan as to how you will go about making the changes. What circumstances make it easiest for you to change? Do you need to find a new job or go back to school so you can get the job you would love?

9. If you feel frozen in place, literally get moving again. You will begin to believe you can take control of your life when you get moving. Go for walks and move your legs and arms. When one man I worked with began spending an hour a day walking in the mall, his life began to move forward again. When you exercise your muscles, beneficial chemicals are released. Breathe deeply and slowly, stand up straight, roll back your shoulders, hold up your head and smile, and you will begin to feel more in control and competent.

Your body language can change your mood. Caesar Milan, television's "Dog Whisperer," gives some great examples involving dogs. When a dog comes to him depressed, with its tail between its legs, Milan literally lifts the tail up. Soon the dog re-engages in life, wagging its tail.

10. Use your imagination. When you get anxious about the trauma, you are usually feeling unsafe. You believe you have little or no control over the situation and the future. Think back to a time you felt safe. Create a safe place to go to in your

Step Eight: Change unwanted behaviors

mind, and strengthen the image to the point you can go there at will whenever you feel threatened. Use all five senses.

For one person, "safety" might mean going into the woods alone. In sandplay therapy, most people see humans as most dangerous, animals less so, and vegetation as least dangerous. However, if your trauma took place in nature, you may see the outdoors as a dangerous place. In that case, choose a different image. One woman who had been sexually abused as a child felt safe only when she imagined herself in the arms of Jesus. She had learned to trust Him implicitly as a child. Even God wouldn't do. She didn't trust a God who had let the trauma happen to her.

STEP NINE:
WORK WITH YOUR EMOTIONS ("ENERGY IN MOTION").

To help you navigate your painful emotions, I suggest you become familiar with the earlier steps and become stable first, before approaching this step. Practice ways to stabilize yourself before you deal with your feelings, if possible. Consider seeing a therapist who can direct and support you through this process safely. In all cases I recommend you arrange to have someone whom you trust available if you need her or him.

What are emotions? They are merely "energy in motion" in your body. But sometimes they can be very powerful, especially if repressed for some time. Often when people think of the word "emotion," their bodies clutch. When they think of a trauma, pain floods their bodies, and they run as far and as fast as they can in the opposite direction.

Is it always essential to remember your past trauma and deal with the emotions it triggers? Not always. For some people, remembering makes them less functional at least for a while, but this is sometimes necessary to go past the trauma. And for some people, their emotions seem overwhelming, and they are terrified of losing control of themselves. You

Step Nine: Work with your emotions ("energy in motion").

will need to be the one to decide if or when you wish to explore your memories and feelings more deeply.

Although I advise not delving into your emotions and traumatic memories until you have stabilized and learned how to change your thinking, following this advice is not always feasible. Some of you have no choice. Your memories and emotions come to greet you without your permission. Your brain won't allow you to wait to get help, even if you would like to. In this case trying to stop the emotions merely makes your symptoms worse.

Many of you have shut down or cut off your emotions after the trauma. To help you act quickly and stay on high alert during a crisis, your body has a wonderful way of numbing out or dissociating so that you can function. Your brain automatically shuts down the feelings you would not otherwise have been able to handle. The problem is that, for most people, the emotions return sooner or later after the crisis is over. Avoiding emotions may work for a while, but not forever.

The power your past trauma holds over you often depends on your avoiding it. According to Dr. Gabor Maté in *When the Body Says No*, in order to be healthy physically, mentally, and emotionally, the energy needs to flow instead of remaining stuck in the body. But you must learn to release your negative emotions in a healthy way so you don't hurt yourself or someone else. Research now indicates that those who can release their anger live on average two years longer than those who can't.

Emotions such as grief, guilt, and anxiety can be very painful, but when you stop them from flowing, other emotions such as joy and happiness usually stop flowing as well. This energy stoppage is what causes the numbness many people feel after a trauma.

In most cases, when the trauma-induced emotions return, you need to deal with them and release them in order to regain normal functioning. The process reminds me of heating water in a pressure cooker. If you close the lid, it may take a little time for the steam to build in the container, but nature determines that the cooker will inevitably explode. Before it does, you have a choice: to turn off the burner and lift the lid at least a little so the steam can slowly escape, or to watch the pot blow up and cause serious damage. In the case of bottled-up emotions, you may try to turn off the burner, but there is something wrong with the stove and it refuses to respond. Now your choice is simple. Carefully, gradually, and with intention lift the lid, or have the pot blow up.

If your emotions keep building until the pot blows up—in other words, you hurt yourself or others—stop running and face your memories and feelings. Don't fight them. Instead, find someone to help you. Then learn how to release the emotions slowly and safely. You will come out at the other end stronger than before.

After Dennis had been shot while in the police force, he and his wife Beverly, came to work with me at Beverly's insistence. They were thinking of getting a divorce, but they had three children, and both members of the couple wanted the marriage to work. Shortly after the session began, Beverly blurted out that she could not handle Dennis's anger anymore. She felt he was becoming dangerous to her and the children. If he refused to deal with his memories, she couldn't stay with him.

Step Nine: Work with your emotions ("energy in motion").

When I glanced at Dennis, I noticed that the words "drugs" and "anger" were large triggers for him. His face turned red. He tapped his foot. Suddenly he got up and raced out the door. Beverly yelled after him, "You said you wouldn't run!" She began to cry. She and I talked for a while, then she made another appointment and left.

Beverly and Dennis did not keep their appointment. I didn't hear from either of them for several weeks. Then one afternoon Dennis called. He and Beverly had separated, but he very much missed his wife and kids. Instead of the anger retreating since their separation, his nightmares, memories, and rages had become worse. He was out of control and no longer able to keep a job or maintain relationships.

At our second session, he decided to face himself and deal with his memories and feelings. It took incredible courage to do this, maybe as much courage as he had shown in the battle with drug dealers when he was shot.

When I asked Dennis what he feared most, he said, "If I face my anger and grief, I will fall apart and be locked up in a mental ward for the rest of my life. I will scream and cry and never stop." Dennis did not fall apart during our time together, although he did spend time crying. Instead he learned to talk about and deal with his pain in a safe way, and his doctor prescribed medications to help him through this difficult process. Yes, occasionally it happens that someone needs to be admitted to the hospital for what some people call a "nervous breakdown," especially after a severe trauma. But with the medications and counseling now available, hospitalization rarely lasts long.

When you fear your emotions so much that you run or suppress them every time they are triggered, you stop growing, and the PTS symptoms worsen. You lose the intimate relationships you had with yourself, your mate, and your loved ones. If this is occurring in your life right now, it may be time to admit reality and accept your feelings.

These are some common emotions people experience when they suffer PTS: ambivalence about life, loneliness, feelings of worthlessness, loss of purpose, depression, grief, guilt and shame, feeling they did something wrong, humiliation over disabilities, frustration and desperation that progress is not occurring quickly enough, self destructive feelings, feelings of abandonment by the people around them especially when those people drop away over time, anger, resentment, powerlessness, and fear about things people don't understand or are not in their control.

Here are specific techniques to deal with some of these more difficult emotions:

For many survivors with PTS or PTSD, there will come a time that the emotions will emerge when you encounter a trigger. Sometimes it occurs so quickly and powerfully, you feel as if you are re-experiencing your trauma. You feel as though you have lost all control, and the rage erupts at anyone that happens to be there at the time, usually your family, spouse, and children. Or you feel guilt, and sadness and immense fear that can immobilize you. You may shake, cry, scream. Remember, emotions are okay. They are merely "energy in motion." It's what you do with them that counts.

When you feel strong emotions, you are not going crazy, but make sure you have someone with you to help you pace

Step Nine: Work with your Emotions ("Energy in Motion").

the rate of release so you remain safe. Usually the feelings will end in minutes, but may recur many times over the next weeks. Think of it like a well you have filled to overflowing and must empty back to a safe level. Eventually the emotions return to where they are manageable.

Many people turn to alcohol and drugs to deal with the pain of their emotions. But don't forget, those emotions are still waiting there like a small bomb, ready to explode if you step on the trigger, regardless of when that occurs. And alcohol, because it is an addictive depressant, will make those feelings worsen over time.

CAUTION: FLOODING

In occasional situations, the emotions continue to surface for hours, sometimes days. If your emotions start to overwhelm you, please call your medical doctor immediately. Trained professionals can help you stem the tide with medications and counseling.

The following are some of the most common emotions and how to cope with them:

ANGER:

When you examine your anger, you will usually find that it is rooted in fear. Many people, especially men, don't like to admit they feel fear, because fear makes them feel helpless and weak. Anger, on the other hand, makes them feel strong and in control. Anger is not a "bad" emotion, as many people believe. It's okay to be angry. Humans are all created with the same emotions, regardless of who they are or where they come from. We were given the emotion of anger for a good reason. It mobilizes and motivates people to act for justice and regain control of their destiny.

However, here is the problem with anger. Responding to threats with aggression, which is normal and often essential to survive in dangerous situations, is not appropriate in everyday life. When you get angry, you may want to lash out and hurt someone or yourself. Don't. What counts is how you act on your anger. **It's the action that becomes the problem, not the emotion.** If you face your anger and engage your logical forebrain, **you have a choice as to how to respond.**

The following are some suggestions to help you with your anger:

1. **Think before you act.**

2. **If you find yourself getting angry and having a hard time controlling yourself, leave immediately.** Make an agreement with family and close friends beforehand, while you are calm. Tell them that at this stage of your recovery you must leave, but you will return to address the problem with them later, when you have calmed down.

3. **Hit something that won't hurt you or someone else.** I had a client who would wear boxing gloves and hit boxes filled with sand. Another client filled a large cloth bag with rolled-up newspapers, hung it in the garage, and hit it with a baseball bat. Another woman who had been sexually abused by her father as a child bought old ceramic dishes at

Step Nine: Work with your emotions ("energy in motion").

a garage sale, took them to the landfill, and smashed them. She needed the sound of the dishes crashing, as well as the physical activity, to let go of her anger.

Release your anger for short periods. Then stop and switch to something you enjoy. The new activity will help you return to the here and now. It is important to make a plan and determine what you would enjoy doing ahead of time, while you are thinking logically.

In a safe place where you are alone and won't frighten anyone, especially your children, smash something that's not important to anyone. Hit or kick a cardboard box, or set up a punching bag. Scream, yell, and cry. Tears often come after the screaming. Tears are normal, and nature's way of releasing stress chemicals from your body.

A different approach might be to go out into the woods, away from everyone, and scream. Pretend the person you are mad at is sitting in front of you, and tell him or her exactly what you feel and how you want the person to be different. All these actions are means to release your emotions safely from your body so you don't hold them inside until you explode. However, some studies now indicate that releasing your anger in this way may in the long run make you more angry. You need to try this out for yourself.

4. Do hard physical activities. These activities must exhaust you enough to release the tension in your muscles. For example, a client who had been attacked began to train for marathons to release her pent-up energy. Here are a few more suggestions to trigger your thinking: sports such as football and soccer, workouts at the gym, running, working on a farm, yard work, construction, martial arts. I'm sure you and your friends can come up with many others. Studying a martial art (judo, karate, etc.) is particularly valuable because you will learn discipline and specific techniques to calm yourself and think before you act. These can also make you feel powerful and in control again, ready in case of any emergency. When I worked at a crisis center we helped people, especially clients who had been raped, to enroll in the martial art of their choosing.

5. After the body releases the emotion, you will feel more relaxed. At this point, ask yourself, "What am I so angry about?" Journal the answer. Then ask yourself, "What am I afraid of? What do I fear I have no control over?" Journal about the fear that triggered the anger, and address the fear as well. Write an angry letter to the person you are mad at, then burn it. Or speak to a counselor or minister about it. Be honest.

Ellen who had been abused by her husband, an Afghanistan war veteran, came to see me for help. She said her husband Jeff would get very angry at her and would hit her if she didn't do exactly what he wanted her to do. I asked her whether she thought Jeff would be willing to come in to see me. A few days later Ellen called to make an appointment for Jeff.

During our session I asked him, "What does she do that makes you so angry?"

He said, "She won't follow orders."

"So what are you afraid will happen if she doesn't follow orders?"

"I'm angry, not scared," he retorted. "I never get scared."

Step Nine: Work with your emotions ("energy in motion").

"Just humor me," I said. "Imagine that you are someone else who does get scared. What might that person be afraid of?"

"I don't know. I guess he'd be scared that he didn't have control over what would happen in his life."

"And what might happen if this man had no control?"

He swallowed hard and said in a quiet voice, "She'd leave me and I'd be all alone. I've already lost all my buddies that I fought with. My friends don't think like I do anymore. My kids don't really want me around. I need her here with me, after all I've been through. I can't handle any more losses."

Jeff's fear underlying his anger dealt with loss—loss of the people in his life, and especially loss of control over others. He felt powerless and out of control over his life. Many veterans face the same issue. Loss of control over your life is indeed often the most frightening loss you will ever face. What are you afraid of losing? Your life or your loved ones life? Love? Closeness? Security? Money?

6. When you are feeling normal again, practice the deep breathing and relaxation exercises described in Step Four so that you can begin to use them the next time you feel angry or anxious. Meditation and prayer have also been found to greatly help reduce feelings of anger.

7. Notice your body when you feel angry. What physical changes take place? Where in your body do you hold your anger? Some people tend to stand straight with head erect, jaws clenched. They feel like forming a fist. Pay attention to what your body does.

8. Take responsibility for your part in the problem. Work on changing your thinking and behavior. Ask yourself, "What do I gain from being angry?"

9. Take life one day at a time. Your anger may get more intense before it weakens. The cardinal rule is to make sure you don't physically or emotionally hurt yourself or others. But all you have is today. So for today, take time to breathe deeply and slowly when you are triggered and remain centered. Then you do the same thing tomorrow. If you mess up, it's okay. Start over again the next day.

FEAR:
Fear is a useful, normal emotion that has kept humans alive over millennia. But if not overcome or dealt with, it can destroy us. In excess it becomes a paranoia, a constant anxiety, or a phobia, making life unmanageable. What you experienced during your trauma is not normal. Most people still believe they must always be strong and that being afraid is not okay. But all people are afraid, and if they don't admit it, they are kidding themselves. That underlying fear, even when you deny it and are not conscious of it, often prevents you from moving on and becoming the person you are capable of becoming. It holds you back from passion and purpose and keeps you from improving your life.

The following are some suggestions to help you deal with fear:

Step Nine: Work with your emotions ("energy in motion").

1. Stop and identify when you are afraid. How does fear feel in your body? Where are you feeling it? What are you thinking?

2. Find a safe place where you can experience it. Let yourself shake, cry, scream, laugh, or whatever lets you experience and move the energy of fear. If you have a dog, you may notice that his entire body shakes when he is afraid, and often he whimpers. After a few minutes, he has released the fear and the shaking stops. It's a normal and healthy way to discharge fear. So make sure you too release the stress from your body after a shock or fearful incident. If you don't, the emotion remains stuck in the body and you may develop tense muscles that can be very painful (e.g., back pain, headaches). Stress affects your immune system and decreases your resistance to disease.

Allow yourself to feel the emotions for about ten minutes. As with anger, it is important not to carry a loaded gun. If you need something to make you feel safe, carry pepper-spray, or carry a very heavy cane made specifically for defense. An FBI agent I met carries a cane everywhere he goes. In airports he pretends he has a limp and no one stops him.

3. Journal. Deal with your fear. Write down what you fear. How logical is your fear? Rethink your fear. Is there really someone out there that wants to hurt you? What can you do to make you feel in more control of your life? (e.g., learn a martial art, solve a problem, etc.).

4. Don't act immediately on your fear. Look at it rationally. Sometimes what happens is that we become so afraid that we begin to lose touch with our principals and deeply held beliefs. We may even be willing to sacrifice freedom, love, justice, and democracy just to be safe. Remember that our forefathers stood firm and refused to allow fear to overcome them. And that's why we have America now. So acknowledge your fear and feel it, but act out of love and reason. When you are afraid, always ask yourself before you act, "Am I acting out of fear?" Then consider how you really wish to act. I asked my father who had come over to Canada as a refugee, whether they had not felt afraid much of the time? He said, "Oh yes. We were terrified, but we didn't act out of that fear. If you act out of fear, Anna, you lose your freedoms and your principles. Then others have control over you."

5. Ponder something you would like to do in your life but haven't done. Ask yourself, "Why don't I do it? What am I afraid of?" To get to the central issue, imagine yourself doing something you fear. Let's say you feel you have nothing in common with your partner anymore and you want to ask her or him to make changes. You are afraid that your partner will be angry and throw you out of the house, or take the kids and everything you own. Or maybe you are afraid s/he will become very depressed and commit suicide.

Journal the following:

- Write down the situation.
- Ask yourself, "What am I afraid would happen if I asked her/him to make changes?"

Step Nine: Work with your emotions ("energy in motion").

- Keep asking, "And then what would happen?" until you have no more answers. Most of the time you will find that you are not nearly as afraid of the end result as you are of the process. Often you will realize that you can handle the process once you get to the end of your fears and see you have choices. Then ask yourself, "What am I afraid will happen if I *don't* ask her/him?" When you face your fears rather than avoid them, frequently you will be motivated to take charge and change your behavior. Your fear dissipates.
- When you have clearly looked at your fear, it is time to deal with the situation. Usually the anger and fear have lessened by then. In the previous example, you could talk to your partner about your fears and feelings. Tell them what they do and how you feel at the time. Take responsibility for your own feelings. No one *makes* you feel a certain way. You might say, "When you're so busy with work and don't take time to do things with me, that triggers my fear. I become afraid we have nothing in common anymore. I love you and I want to work on a solution together."

SADNESS AND GRIEF:
Sadness and grief occur when we lose something or someone, and also when we **think** we have lost something. A loss of belief, especially in a moral value we hold dear, can be as damaging as a physical loss.

Have you lost your mobility due to an injury? Have you lost your clear thinking? Your mate and children? Your friendships? Your purpose in life? Your beliefs of invulnerability and that justice always prevails?

After a loss, or the fear of an imminent loss, most of us experience a period of denial. Our bodies and emotions become numb and our minds say, "This isn't happening." That's so we can handle the shock of the loss, or death and disaster, shortly after it occurs. But later the normal process of grieving continues. Next, most people become angry. "Why did this have to happen to me? There is no justice. How could God let this happen?" But sometimes sadness and tears, not anger, come soon after a loss. All you want to do is cry and hide.

Many people begin to bargain with God. Let's say you were wounded in an accident and the doctor has told you he will have to remove your arm. You plead, "Please, God, if you just save my arm, I will go to church every week," or "I'll volunteer to help needy people." But since there is no way to save both the arm and your life, the doctor removes the arm.

Suddenly you realize what you have lost. You will never do many of the things you used to enjoy. You will never return to the construction job you had before you were injured. Hopelessness and depression set in. In most cases it may well take a year to resolve and accept your loss. Sometimes acceptance takes much longer. Don't get discouraged. This is the normal process of recovering from grief. You will need support from others as well as psychotherapy if the grief is too prolonged.

Here are some suggestions to help you deal with grief and loss:

STEP NINE: WORK WITH YOUR EMOTIONS ("ENERGY IN MOTION").

1. Allow your emotions to surface. Release them in a safe way. Some people get stuck in depression because they stop the anger and sadness. When your tears flow, the energy in your body begins to flow as well. People often feel as though their tears are endless, or that it is weak to cry. That's what most of us have been taught in our culture. But tears are normal and need to be released. They will stop when you have emptied the well enough not to overflow. Tears have been designed by nature to release your stress chemicals. Most people say they feel more calm and at peace after crying.

2. Journal about what happened and about your feelings. Keep the energy flowing.

3. Attend groups that deal with loss. A group that has similar issues to yours may be your best option at this point because the people there will understand how you feel and will probably be most supportive.

4. Change your thinking and behavior. Change your thinking and soon your emotions will change (see Step Seven on changing your thinking). When emotions arise, ask yourself what you were thinking at the time. This is a conscious urgent moment. Listen and acknowledge what you hear. They are powerful statements coming from within you. They are there to tell you something you need to know to heal, before you deny the emotions again. You will likely have to look at the trauma and break down your fear of the memory before you can start thinking about it differently.

GUILT AND SHAME:
Survivor guilt is beautifully expressed in this section of Patrick Overton, a Vietnam veteran's poem, "The Healing Wall":

Then I began to move my hands over the Wall–
over names I did not know, slow at first, and then faster, almost frantically–
at first not knowing why
but then knowing
I was looking for one name,
I was looking for the one groove my hands
would know the best,
the one that would confirm what I always knew
to be true but was afraid to admit
a name that wasn't there but should have been mine..
..........the source of my guilt, my one great sin
I had lived. I had come home.
I was no more deserving than any one of these names,
but I had survived.

Guilt and shame, frequently related, are common in survivors especially when other people have been involved in the trauma. You may feel you did something wrong and you feel guilt and shame about what you did or didn't do. Or maybe you feel guilty that you can't fully be the parent your children need.

A teenager I saw felt enormous guilt for surviving when her friend died in the accident they were in when a drunk driver suddenly swerved into them. Although she was not to

Step Nine: Work with your emotions ("energy in motion").

blame for the crash, she felt she should have somehow been able to avoid what happened. She would often say to me, "If only I had. . ." and "Why didn't I . . ."

Even children who have been abused physically or sexually often feel they were somehow to blame and they carry a great deal of shame about what happened to them. Many still have those same feelings as adolescents and adults.

It's hard to move on when you carry a great deal of guilt and shame. Ask yourself, "Was I really in control of what happened?" If the answer is no, drop your guilt. You are not responsible. Remember, children are never to blame for abuse. They are incapable of protecting themselves. If the answer is yes, ask yourself? "Why did I do what I did? Was it because I didn't take the time to consider all the facts? Did I have the time? Did I have all the facts? Did I do it out of fear? Did I mean to hurt someone? Or did I do it deliberately out of self-interest and anger? What was my motivation?" The truth is that we cannot predict the outcome of our actions. We make decisions on what we know at the time, and most of the time they turn out okay. But then once in a while... they don't. Why? No one knows.

It is essential that you be honest and admit to yourself what really happened. Make amends if you are responsible, then forgive yourself. If you did it out of fear, you will need to admit that you, like everyone else, is human. Fear can be an intense and overwhelming human emotion.

Here are some ways to deal with guilt and shame:

1. Journal about what happened.

2. Journal what your feelings and thoughts were at the time.

3. If you believe you did something wrong, admit it to yourself and to at least one other person whom you trust. Maybe that person will be your priest, rabbi, minister, or spiritual advisor, maybe a close nonjudgmental friend or a counselor.

4. Make amends to the people you wronged, if they are alive and if it is possible to contact them. If they are not alive or you are unable to contact them, write them a letter and ask their forgiveness. Read it out loud. Then burn it. Burning is an important symbol of letting go for most people.

5. Ask for forgiveness in any way you need to and write yourself a forgiveness letter.

Audrey, one of the women I counseled, had struggled for several years to forgive herself for having an abortion as a teenager. She could not come to peace with what she had done. I knew she attended the local Catholic church regularly and I also knew the priest. When I asked Audrey whether it would be okay for me to contact Father Tom, she hesitated, then said, "Yes." Father Tom called Audrey the next day, and they met at the church. After Father Tom talked to Audrey and granted her forgiveness, Audrey finally let go of her guilt and moved on.

The Healing Wall, Part III

by Patrick Overton, Ph.D. and Vietnam veteran

I was becoming part of the Wall, or the Wall part of me.
The more I tried to move away, the more I couldn't move.
It began to pull out of me
emotions I had not felt since I was there,
since that first moment I saw and knew
I had been part of someone's death-
reliving the moment of lost innocence,
remembering the emptiness,
feeling again, the sickness in my heart
I had kept numb for years.
That is when the first tear came, and then a second,
followed by more-
Slow tears, warm tears from down deep inside the hole of me.
I became a prisoner of the Wall, captive by its silent,
vigilant, roll call of death.

STEP TEN:
Reconnect spiritually.

In this section I am not referring to any specific religious or spiritual beliefs. I speak of God or "spirit" or "creative force" as a power greater than our human ego selves.

Various traumas, especially ones such as abuse, school shootings, and war are considered by many to be a moral issue and a "soul trauma" as well as a physical, emotional, and mental one. Although some survivors have not lost their belief in a loving spiritual being, many others question their faith. Why would a loving God allow the hatred, destruction, suffering, and death and not intervene? Why has God deserted us? Why did the creator of everything not make the world and humanity better than this? Does the Creator not care about us? Does this higher power even exist?

Human induced traumas often deliver a deep soul wound to the survivors' identities, senses of morality, and relationships to society. They may feel abandoned, depressed, and angry at God. They have lost their sense of purpose and their reason for being on Earth. Many of these feelings come from the emptiness of not being spiritually connected, of having lost trust and faith in a higher power.

Step Ten: Reconnect spiritually.

Combat veterans often deal with the deepest spiritual soul pain. In an article in *Clinical Psychological Review* (December 2009), VA psychologist Bret Litz and his colleagues wrote that the greatest lasting harm to veterans comes from moral injury and guilt, especially survivor guilt. This is true of others as well who have survived when the people around them died. He or she may wonder, "Why was I one of the people who survived, when others didn't?"

Many veterans also have the guilt of killing or harming others. Regardless of which religion you may have been raised in, or which spiritual path you have taken, most shun taking human life unless absolutely necessary. The messages you received in your house of worship and your society are often directly in opposition to what you have been required to do in war, creating a tremendous internal moral struggle. One of the veterans I spoke to recently kept repeating the question, "How do I reconcile what I learned in my church and at home with what my culture and government needed me to do? The reality is that war is hell. Did I make the right decisions, or should I have done things differently? It hurts me inside all the time."

An individual with physical and emotional injuries may be left to create a new identity and a new lifestyle. If you want to connect or reconnect with and trust a higher power again, how do you do it?

Here are some suggestions:

1. Meditation and prayer. I won't give you a definition of prayer or meditation. You need to define these words for yourself. Some people see meditation and prayer as two sides of a coin, defining meditation as a way to empty their minds of all thoughts and allow their higher power to speak to them, and prayer as a way for them to speak to their higher power.

Recently neurologists have discovered a small area in the brain that is activated when people meditate or pray, allowing people to experience their spirituality. The amygdala (emotional brain) calms down, and the pathways in a certain area in the brain open up and connect with something higher than their ordinary self. Meditation and prayer also opens people up to love and compassion for themselves and everyone around them.

I suggest that the most powerful way to meditate and pray is in a group, especially in a circle that connects you with people who care about one another, who can understand what you are going through, and who show compassion to one another. For many of you, prayer and meditation may remind you that you are connected to something greater than just you. It will often help you to see a bigger picture of what you have experienced and the purpose of what happened.

2. Let go. Use the first three steps of a twelve-step program to help you let go of needing to be in control of everything that happens to you. Attend a 12 step program such as AA or Alanon. Although at present, to my knowledge, there are no twelve-step programs specific to PTSD, clients often adapt the twelve steps to better serve their situation. The following is a possible version of the first three steps, as mentioned in the AA Big Book.

Step Ten: Reconnect Spiritually.

- We admitted we were powerless over our situation and that our lives had become unmanageable.
- Came to believe that a power greater than ourselves could restore us to sanity.
- Made a decision to turn our will and our lives over to the care of our higher power as we understand that higher power.

3. Write down in your journal what you have believed in the past, and what you believe now. Who are you? What are your moral and ethical beliefs and core values? What is your worldview? What do you think mankind's purpose is here on earth? What is the meaning of life? What is your purpose in being here?

4. Visit a religious house of worship or join a spiritual group. Talk to a spiritual advisor of your choice who will listen to you and empathize as well as give you advice. Remember: It is better not to get caught up in the dogma. Rules and regulations are important but they are mostly established by humans.

5. Read spiritual literature that is uplifting and inspirational. Judgmental books are not for you at this point. Look on the Internet and in church libraries, public libraries, and bookstores. Ask counselors, friends, and other people who also have PTS for recommendations of books they have found valuable.

6. Create a ritual. Meditate and/or pray at least three times a day, even for short periods, such as a few minutes. Before you meditate be clear and ask your higher consciousness for specific answers to the issues you are dealing with at this time. Lie down in a comfortable place with no distractions and direct your focus onto your breath. I like to lie on the grass under a tree in a quiet place and put all my worries onto a cloud and send it away.

You can close your eyes or concentrate on a blank white wall. Take slow deep breaths in through your nose and out through your mouth. Notice the sound of your breath, the feeling in your chest, and any smells and sounds. Imagine seeing your breath filling your lungs and then deflating until all your daily thoughts fade into the distance and your mind is blank. This state is very restful to the mind and body. Sometimes you receive great insights and often you get answers to your problems and your questions.

You can also think of a "mountaintop" experience you have had and meditate on it. Some people have had special dreams or visions, out-of-body experiences, or even near-death experiences. If you've ever had such encounters, treasure them and hang on to the feeling they gave you. Bring them back often.

7. Several times a day, speak to a personal God (higher power) who is listening to you and cares about you. Create an image of God in your mind. What does your God look like? A cloud? A light? A man? A woman? Tell God your problems. Start by trusting God just a little, if that's all you can do. One of my clients quoted Matthew 17:20, the verse in

Step Ten: Reconnect Spiritually.

the Bible that says that if you have faith as small as a mustard seed you will be able to move mountains. He said, "A mustard seed. That's pretty small. I think I can do that."

8. Resolve your shame and guilt. If you feel at fault for something that happened and think that you "are not good enough," ask yourself, "Was I in control of the situation?" If not, let the guilt go. It's not yours to carry.

When you feel shame, you think you let yourself and others down, and all you want to do is withdraw. Don't. Face your shame and guilt. If you were in control of what happened and you **chose** to do something that hurt others, be honest about your mistakes and take responsibility for them. Take an honest moral inventory of what you have done in the past and own your mistakes. But you are not at this place now. Separate the past from the present. Then send deep understanding and love to that part of you. Share the inventory with someone who will understand. Shame dissipates when you feel understood and you receive empathy. Then ask for forgiveness and make amends.

But apologizing and asking for forgiveness is of little value if you don't change your behavior. I imagine most of you know or have heard of someone who, after being caught in a negative behavior, followed all the steps above and apologized, but did not change his/her behavior. Instead the person kept doing what s/he had always done, so the apologies meant little.

Also know that sometimes shame and guilt are positive emotions. When you feel them, you know that you have a conscience. This is good. In the bigger view of life, our consciences shape social behavior and help our communities and species survive.

9. Forgive yourself and others. Forgiveness is possible. Here is another issue all of us must face. Inside each of us there is what we call a "light side" and a "dark side." One of the clients I met with was the wife of a Vietnam veteran. She said that her husband could not forgive himself for allowing that dark side to come out while at war. He could not forgive himself for killing and torturing people, for burning villages, and for walking away from screaming children and women. He spent a lot of time muttering in his sleep and talking to God. But he could not believe that God could forgive him for what he had done. He could not *accept* the forgiveness of God. Forty years later, he is still sure he will spend eternity in hell. Another one of my clients could not forgive herself for not protecting her mother from domestic violence. Another one could not forgive herself for not protecting her younger sister from sexual abuse.

How can you forgive yourself?

- **Accept that you are human and have limitations.** As I've said, fear can immobilize anyone. It is normal to be afraid especially when your life is threatened. Instead of becoming defensive and isolated, admit that you were afraid. Now visualize that frightened person in your mind and give it love instead of berating it.

Step Ten: Reconnect Spiritually.

Humans have both light and dark sides. The truth is that when you live with continual violence such as in an abusive home or neighborhood and are often afraid for your life, the dark side may come out. Anger, hatred, violence, and even torture can be the results. If you wish the dark side to stop coming out at the most inopportune times, you will need to forgive and learn to love even that side of yourself.

- **Confess to another person what you did,** someone you trust who won't judge you, like a close friend, a fellow survivor, minister, priest, or rabbi. Acknowledge what you believe you did wrong, first to yourself, then to a spiritual advisor, and ask for forgiveness.
- **Allow others to love you, hug you, and forgive you.** Allow yourself to accept the forgiveness of your higher power and of others. Open your heart and let in the light—the feelings of forgiveness.
- **Cultivate your "light side."** Show compassion and love for others and yourself, and allow your actions now and in the future to come out of love instead of fear. Do random acts of kindness daily. Before you act, give yourself permission to think for a moment and make a conscious choice about how you will act. What do you wish your motivation to be? Fear? Anger? Love? Showing kindness can be as simple as helping someone cross the street or smiling at him or her.
- **Ask your higher power to forgive you.** Most religions believe that their higher power is always open to forgiving people who are sincere. Envision your higher power standing in front of you. Dialogue with

that benevolent wise being. Ask him/her/it for forgiveness and imagine that entity forgiving you. Then allow forgiveness into your heart. Feel the burden you have been carrying lift.
- **Now it is time to forgive yourself.** Visualize your dark side standing near you and talk to it. Repeat "I forgive myself" out loud or in your mind, many times a day. Give yourself compassion. Often we forgive others but tend not to forgive ourselves. You are just as important as anyone else.
- **Write yourself a forgiveness letter and read it out loud every day, especially just before you go to bed.**
- **Take time to ask yourself the following questions:** What have you gained from adversity? What would you do differently next time? What is the worst thing that could happen to you if you gave up your guilt? What did you learn?

10. Create an altar or a sacred space. Discover what helps you feel more spiritual and closer to your higher power. If you have come from a church or religion that uses some kind of incense, your sense of smell may be your connection. Music or chanting is another way to connect. Practice reassuring rituals. One of the men I worked with returned to his native culture to attend rituals and to do a vision quest. He said it helped him regain his purpose and reason for living. He is now much less depressed and is moving in a new direction.

You might use paintings, pictures, statuary, or anything else tangible that is important to you. Flowers and plants are alive and will move you to feeling alive. Place them

Step Ten: Reconnect Spiritually.

somewhere you consider to be a special place in your house. The altar will help reconnect you to your higher self whenever you need it.

Some of my clients have created small trays with some sand in it. They add important objects and pictures into the trays and create a scene. They rearrange the objects, remove some or add others whenever they wish.

Create some form of art (see Step Fourteen) and place it on the altar. Art often expresses a spiritual component of ourselves. It seems to me that any artistic expression, when motivated by spiritual compassion, will bring out your soul, will live in your creation, and will touch and heal you and others.

When I asked a friend who was raped in the military, "What helped you most during your recovery?" she said without hesitation, "My daily Buddhist practice."

Here is what she wrote:

Buddhism as a Spiritual Path and Practice
For this woman veteran with a
Post Traumatic Stress driven life
Helped me to salvage
My one precious life.

Satya planted the seed for understanding
How to practice compassion
A most rewarding and difficult path
Learning how to Love you and me more
In our eternal now.

G. Maeve Aeolus, Vietnam Veteran, RN, C

In her ardent search for recovery and resilience after being raped in the military and having continuous suicidal thoughts, Maeve has finally found relief and peace in her spiritual connection.

STEP ELEVEN:
DEAL WITH MEMORIES.

A word of warning for people with severe PTS: memories often set off emotions that trigger a reliving of the trauma. If you are at home and need to deal with your memories, call someone you trust who can help you in case you need her or him. Ask the person to stay with you, if possible, until the memories have passed. If you are in a 12 step program ask your sponsor to be with you.

IF YOU, LIKE MANY SURVIVORS, feel compelled to repeat your story over and over again in an attempt to master the event, don't let people tell you that there is something wrong with you. This "need to tell" your memories and have someone witness what happened to you is common and normal, and can be very helpful. As a matter of fact, telling your story is one of two kinds of therapy found to be most effective in healing PTSD. Talking helps your mind release the memory of the trauma and rebuild it or change it.

Until recently, scientists have not fully understood what happens in your brain when you retell your trauma, except that the heightened emotional energy charge in the amygdala is decreased. But new research has also revealed that memory is much more complex than previously believed. It was once thought memory did not change. While it was obvious that people had different perceptions of an event, it was believed that once that memory was seared into the brain, it did not change, even after many retellings.

Then in 1999 Dr. Karim Nader discovered that memory was not nearly as stable as people thought. He and others showed that reactivating a memory by remembering or retelling it actually destabilized it, placing it into a flexible state where it could be permanently altered.

Each time you remember or retell your memories, they change. Amazing! It is now obvious why remembering and retelling can be so powerful, both for the negative and the positive. The following suggestions are meant to give you ways of dealing with your emotions, but also ways to remember, retell, and rebuild your memory of your trauma in a more positive and less traumatizing way.

If possible work through Step One on stabilization and Step Seven on changing your thinking before you continue with Step Eleven. Journaling can bring up powerful memories. You need to recognize common symptoms of PTS and how you can handle them when you feel unstable. Practice your breathing and relaxation techniques (Step Four) to calm you while you journal or remember.

The following are a few suggestions on how to deal with your memories:

1. Write in a journal. Many people have told me that journaling their memories and feelings has been the most effective therapy for them. Writing helps release the feelings and

Step Eleven: Deal with memories.

memories from the brain instead of allowing them to continue swirling and enlarging. It is best to journal daily, as well as whenever the trauma comes to mind or you feel a strong emotion. Some people carry their journals with them wherever they go, even to work or school.

- Begin by journaling your feelings as often as you can. You can journal about all your emotions, also positive ones, such as happiness, joy, and contentment.

    Here is an example: Write, "I am feeling so angry right now. . . ." and continue to tell what you are angry about and what happened to trigger this anger. Maybe you will refer back to the trauma, and maybe you won't. That's not important. What is important is getting your feelings down on paper.
- If the emotion takes over, express it in a safe way (see Step Nine). After you have expressed your feelings, you may want to diffuse them by checking what other emotions lay underneath the obvious ones. For example, when you look closely at anger, you may find that you are afraid of something. Ask yourself, "What am I afraid of?" It may be fear of having no control over the situation. Loss of control is very frightening and is one of the main symptoms of PTS. If your partner says or does something you don't like and you get angry and blow up, ask yourself why. The situation might upset you because you can't control what is happening and what the consequences of that action will be. Maybe underneath you're afraid that he or she will leave you.

- List what you can do to improve your situation. In our example, rather than yell at your partner, you could sit down quietly and tell him or her what you are feeling. Then ask for his or her point of view, and work together to find a solution to your problem. If that doesn't work, see whether the two of you can seek counseling together. (More techniques for problem solving and decision making are discussed in Step Three.)
- Look at your part in the problem, write it down in your journal, and decide what you want to change. Remember, you can't change other people's behaviors, but you can change your own. When one person changes, usually the other person's response will change as well. Patterns of behavior develop over time as they are repeated. You may have observed and learned these patterns in your family while you were growing up. Do you usually respond in anger to certain problems, blow up, and then blame your partner for what happened? Or do you withdraw? Experiment with handling the problem differently. Set your anger or fear aside with your rational mind, listen to your loved one and then accept your part in the pattern.
- What lesson, if any, can you learn from what happened? Journal about it. Recognizing the lessons you can learn by going through hard times is difficult at first, but becomes easier as you go along. Maybe you learned you really do have more control over yourself than you thought. Maybe you learned that thinking

Step Eleven: Deal with memories.

before you act on your feelings helps you get what you need. Maybe you learned that you are more compassionate now than ever before.

- If you are able, place yourself in the shoes of the other person. Ask yourself how he or she might be feeling and why. Often he or she is also afraid of something. Again, write it down.

Several years ago my daughter studied ballet with a prima ballerina from Hungary. After each class, my daughter came home angry. Mrs. Blumenthal (not her real name) had yelled at the girls again. "You all look like cows! Won't you ever learn?" Now, keep in mind that the girls she was teaching were all exceptional dancers, most heading toward careers in dance. My daughter and her friends, afraid of losing their positions in the company, refused to speak up. I told my daughter that her instructor's behavior probably had little to do with what the girls were doing, but my daughter had difficulty believing she was not an inferior dancer in some way.

One day I sat down with her and we came up with a plan of how to handle the situation. We spent time finding out about Mrs. Blumenthal's life in Hungary under Communist rule and her escape to America. Suddenly the yelling and need for control made sense to my daughter. Although she could not change the situation, she had changed her perspective. Instead of anger, she felt empathy and sadness toward her instructress. Her relationship with Mrs. Blumenthal changed almost immediately.

When I asked my daughter what she had learned, she said, "Two things: I'll never treat my students that way, and I will look underneath to see what's going on with the other person whom I'm having problems with." She and another woman now own a dance company, and she lives what she learned.

2. Retell your trauma story. This technique is one that therapists have learned can be very effective in trauma recovery, when the person is ready. It may take time before you feel ready to tell your story. There is no need to rush. The goal is to reduce and manage your anxiety and fears. Retelling your story many times over usually lessens your reaction to your trauma and defuses the intensity of the memory. It breaks certain networks and connections in the brain.

After a while, you will be able to face the trauma without a severe bodily and emotional reaction. Telling your story usually helps you direct your anger at the right target (e.g., your abuser), not at your loved ones. Furthermore, the anger and fear will disperse over time. You will also find that your story evolves and if you can add new facts and different perspectives to what happened your memories will change. Did someone come to help you? Were you thankful you survived? How has your life changed in positive ways as well because of the trauma? Have you gained wisdom? For instance, do you have more empathy for people now than you had? Do you want to help others who have been traumatized?

I remember times when my father needed to share his memories of war. They would begin to tumble out of his mouth whenever he remembered. At the time, most people

Step Eleven: Deal with memories.

around him, including my mother, were terrified of negative emotions, especially anger, and they silenced him. He stopped speaking of his memories entirely, but that did not stop his outbursts of anger. Only now the outbursts were directed at the family, instead of at what he had witnessed as a refugee and in the war.

If your memories trigger your emotions to such an extent that you are having difficulty functioning, you must see a therapist who can guide you through this process. Always start by telling yourself that **the incident that triggered the trauma is in the past. You survived and you are safe now.** You don't need to be afraid of your memories. They are just that: memories. Record your stories on a digital recorder as you tell them. Replay them later and you will see how your story has evolved over time.

- Tell your story to a therapist or a trusted friend. Although repeating your story over and over again may not always be necessary to recovery, many people have found that each time they recount the trauma to someone they trust, the impact of the trauma lessens. When you talk to someone you trust, tell the person that you don't need advice. You just need him or her to listen. The energy from the emotion dissipates further each time you tell your memory. Sharing your story also helps you make sense of what happened and reveals what you can learn from the experience.
- Tell your story to an animal like your dog or cat or horse. They will always accept and love you. And they have an uncanny way of knowing exactly what

you need. When I was deeply in grief after my husband's death I often told my dog what I was feeling. He would sit next to me, look into my eyes, and lick my tears.

- If there is no one around to whom you can tell your story, journal it. Many of my clients say that journaling was the most important step in their recovery.
- Attend group therapy, such as a VA or a mental health group, church group, twelve-step program, or online group on the Internet. As humans we need to have someone witness our feelings and to feel accepted, regardless of what we have done or what has happened to us. At the same time, avoid telling your stories to people who may judge you or join you in your depression, fears, or anger. Select a group with a positive leader and other individuals who will encourage you as well as commiserate with you. In a healthy group, you should feel supported and have a better outlook on life by the time you leave.
- A word of caution: If you find telling your story over and over makes you more depressed or angry and that you are unable to let go of the feelings and are beginning to use the story to increase your anger or to get sympathy from others, make sure you see a psychotherapist to help you get past your trauma and heal.

3. Maintain prolonged contact with the environment and/or situation that triggers you, via your imagination. With a technique called Prolonged Exposure Therapy (PET), used effectively for many years to help people overcome phobias,

Step Eleven: Deal with memories.

a person confronts her or his fears in a safe environment, either in the imagination or in the real world. The goal is to decrease your fears and to reinforce that you, not your memories, are in control of your life. The process must be done step-by-step if it is going to help you learn to overcome your fear of a place or situation. PET works best if you begin with a lesser fear and gradually work up to the major trauma.

In "the good old days," we used to tell people to "buck up," to jump back on the proverbial horse after falling off. For example, if as a child you couldn't swim and you almost drowned, a parent might have thrown you back into the ocean to make you face your fears immediately. Well, sometimes the results of this "tough love" were positive, but often they were catastrophic. For many, the practice etched the fear more deeply into the brain, turning it into a phobia almost impossible to extinguish.

If fear is limiting your life and you want to recover, you cannot ignore it. I have dealt with several people who were unable to leave their homes, to walk into a crowded place, or to sit near a door or window for fear of attack. They felt exposed and vulnerable. Some moved into the mountains or the forest to get away from people altogether.

If you choose to use this immersion technique, here are some suggestions:

a. **Imagine the environment you fear.** Many survivors who were severely stressed find they are afraid of, or at least very uncomfortable with, specific places. These can be closed spaces like elevators and unfamiliar buildings, or open ones like roads and streets. Or they may experience other fears, such as social phobias: leaving the house, being in crowds, being cornered, sitting near doors and windows, and hearing loud noises like a car backfiring or a fireworks display. Although you may not always consciously remember why, these places and events can trigger you back to your trauma.

Here is an example of how to help extinguish the fear by using your imagination. Let's say you are afraid of being in a room with many people, and therefore have given up attending social events, but this is a behavior you'd like to change.

- First find a safe space where you can relax and won't be disturbed. Take some time to check in with yourself to understand why the situation triggers you back to the fear of the trauma. Were you in a crowded place at the time or were you in a closed space where you couldn't escape? Write about it in your journal.
- Now imagine standing outside a crowded room or party, looking in from a distance, far enough away to feel safe. Talk to yourself. Remind yourself that you are in a safe place now.
- Repeat this exercise over several days. Each time, imagine and journal about moving closer and closer to the party until you actually walk inside. Each day, write down what you are feeling in your body as you approach. Does your heart pound? Are you perspiring? Are your legs shaking?
- When you can imagine being in the party without wanting to scream and leave, then imagine yourself talking to people and enjoying the event.

Step Eleven: Deal with memories.

Reaching this level of comfort may take several days or even weeks. Don't get discouraged. You are moving forward.
- When you are ready, actually attend a function with just a few people. The next time, add more people. If you need to leave, don't be discouraged. Simply continue the imagining and journaling until the fear gradually dissipates. Your fears will shrink as your mind realizes that a crowded room no longer represents danger.
- Most of us are afraid of change but the more often we do something the easier it becomes. When you feel you've conquered one fear, then choose a more pressing fear to work on and repeat the same sequence of steps. Remember, progress most often takes place outside your comfort zone.

An emerging technology for trauma survivors called virtual reality may help people in the future process their feelings. You or your therapist punches in the particulars and the machine creates a similar reality and environment you were in when the trauma occurred. At present virtual reality equipment is being installed in many Veterans Affairs therapy rooms. Of course, it is best to use these programs in conjunction with psychotherapy. Read Step Nineteen to learn more about this and other groundbreaking new technologies.

b. Maintain prolonged contact with actual triggering environments: This is called the "real-world practice" approach, based on the idea that the easiest way to lose your fear is to actually experience the environment you fear. But unlike the thrown-in-the-ocean example cited above, the fear-producing environment should be experienced gradually, a little at a time, so as not to overwhelm you and worsen your fears. Slowly and over several days, reintroduce yourself to traumatic environments, as you did in your imagination in the previous exercise. Journal your reactions. Use deep breathing and relaxation exercises when you need to. Often this technique is better done with a therapist or another person you trust rather than alone, in case your memories trigger you and flood you with emotions.

Francis, who had been pinned down under a beam during a house fire panicked each time she even imagined herself in a confined space. She worked on the third floor of an office building and lived in a fifth floor apartment but could no longer take the elevator without experiencing a panic attack. She walked up and down the stairs each time without too much difficulty. But then she injured her leg. Although she wanted to be independent, she quit her job and moved back in with her parents. That's when she came in to see me. Using prolonged exposure therapy, she was able to slowly get back into an elevator and after a couple of months went back to work.

4. Release your trauma memories symbolically. Our minds constantly work with symbols. For each person, these symbols may be different. A dog means love to me, and I feel warm and happy inside when I see one. But to someone else who was bitten as a child, a dog may be frightening. A snake

STEP ELEVEN: DEAL WITH MEMORIES.

reminds me of the garter snakes I grew up with on our ranch in central Canada. I think they are slithery, but certainly not frightening. To someone else who lived in an area with rattlesnakes, snakes are terrifying. Different religions and cultures use symbols as well. In a Christian church, the cross symbolizes Christ's crucifixion. In Western culture, a wedding band symbolizes a person's commitment to her or his partner. Rituals and ceremonies can be used to mark a life change or transition, allowing a person to let go of the old and move into the new. Native Americans use many such ceremonies. In the Jewish faith, a bar mitzvah symbolizes the passage of a boy into manhood.

Some people, when they are ready to move on, toss their outmoded or outgrown symbols into a stream or river and watch them float away. They don't need them anymore. Others use burning as a way to release and let go. In some cases, such as when you decide to let go of an angry letter you have written to someone, you are glad to burn that symbol. But many times the ceremony may let go of a symbol and a time that you once cherished or are still grieving (e.g., a death or relationship), but you know that it's time to move on.

You are safe now. It is time to leave your trauma behind and move forward in your life, time to let go of the trauma memories and create new ones. Here are a few suggestions to help you let go, but you are the only one who knows what your personal symbols are, and what they mean to you, and when you are ready to release them.

- If you are a policeman/woman, a fireman, a veteran, an ambulance worker, a nurse and wore a uniform,

respectfully pack it and place it somewhere safe. It's not that you aren't proud of your service, but the act signals that you are ready to move on into a new life. Buy some new clothes that indicate who you are now.
- Write down, then burn your stories of your trauma experiences, fears, pain, resentments, and anger. Or throw the papers into the river and watch them float away.
- Create a new symbol—one that reminds you that you have survived and are growing in strength and compassion. That may be a photo of yourself in new clothes, posed with family and loved ones or a favorite pet, or at a job you enjoy. As you look at the photo frequently, your mind will gradually incorporate this new image of yourself.
- Celebrate your new life. The celebration can include anything from hosting a gathering of friends to going off alone to the forest to listen to the wind in the trees, or to a brook flowing through a meadow.

5. **Change your memories of the trauma.** What do you choose to focus on in your memory? You have a choice. Your memories depend very much on your perception of the event that occurred, which might differ from someone else's perception. Do you ever compare your childhood memories with those of a parent, brother, sister, or friend? Your memories will likely differ from theirs, even though each of you experienced the same event, because everyone focused on different aspects of that event. Each of us remembers our own stories in the context of what was happening to us at the time.

Step Eleven: Deal with memories.

Interestingly, when you incorporate new facts about the event, your memories will change as well. For example, maybe you are angry at your father for something he did when you were a child. If you find out that your father was very ill that day, or that your father came from an abusive home, you won't think of him in the same way as you did in the past. Your feelings of compassion will make you less judgmental of him. In the case of trauma memories, imagine that you talk to another person who knows the person who hurt you and she tells you your abuser was beaten severely as a child and abandoned. Would having that additional knowledge change your feelings? I don't know, but for many of you it might.

Scientists such as Dr. Joseph LeDoux from New York University and his research team have recently discovered that as you replay your memories, you reawaken and recombine them as many times as you remember that particular event. Unknowingly (or sometimes knowingly), you add new details and tweak the facts. Each time you remember the event, you replace that version with a slightly different one, until all you can recall is the new version of your original memory.

Because memories change each time you remember them, you are able to make them more or less traumatic, depending on how you choose to see them. Rebuilding your memories using different data or perceptions about the event will eventually change your feelings. Now you have a choice as to how and what you want to remember about your trauma.

The most important question you need to ask yourself is, "Where is my focus when I remember my trauma?" Do you focus on all the terrible events that happened? That's the case for most people. But what if you chose to remember some good things as well? What if you also remembered someone coming to rescue you, or someone supporting you during the tragedy? Were you aware of anyone trying to help you? Where were you injured—could things have been worse? Remind yourself that you survived. Picture your mate or friends praying for you, and being there for you during your recovery. You can see the goodness of mankind and the world as well. Even though nothing had changed, one of my clients who learned that her neighbor had reported the abuse she had suffered at the hands of her family looked at her trauma differently. Someone had cared enough to try to help.

Several techniques work to change or reconsolidate a memory of a trauma, and thereby alter the emotions associated with it. One is called rebuilding your memories.

Here is a way to begin using this technique:

- **Do some research about your traumatic event** and incorporate any new facts you learn that you didn't know back then. Check with other people who were present or involved in the event. What might they have seen or understood that you didn't? Are there any new facts (e.g., about the brain) that you can include in your memory and choose to focus on the next time you remember?

  Jordon, who was seriously injured during a fall climbing a mountain in Montana, felt he had been left to die without help. He lay there for what seemed a very long time and eventually drifted into unconsciousness. Several hours later, he woke up and realized

Step Eleven: Deal with memories.

he had been airlifted to a medical facility. Though his physical injuries were severe, the most painful part of his memory was the belief that his friends who knew where he would be had not tried to rescue him. He felt abandoned. Soon after the accident his family from another state, took him home to a hospital near them and Jordon didn't communicate with his friends for a while. His memories continued to haunt him.

When he finally e-mailed his friends and got their take on the story, he found their perceptions were very different from his. They told him that they had tried several times to rescue him, but had been unable to get near him and had left him to get help. They felt immense guilt and shame at letting him down. Jordon now remembers the story of his trauma very differently from how he once did.

- Remember your trauma as you originally experienced it. Journal it, or re-experience it by telling it to someone else. Then, at least ten minutes, but no longer than two hours later (the period when the brain rebuilds the memory, according to Dr. LeDoux's research team), remember the trauma again. At this time incorporate the new facts, thoughts, and feelings that you've discovered about the event. Remember that you survived. Also include what you have learned. When you have completed the exercise, write the new version down and reread it several times. From now on, when you remember the trauma and tell it to someone else, always include the updated account.

STEP TWELVE:
Take responsibility for yourself. You have choices.

After a trauma people often feel that they no longer belong in their circle of friends and their families and that they have lost all purpose or control over their lives. They become anxious and depressed.

It is very easy at this point to continue feeling and acting as a victim long after the event has passed. In order to heal and become resilient you must take responsibility for yourself again. Remember, feelings and thoughts will come and go, and you can work on changing them. As we discussed earlier, you can choose where you focus your thoughts. Ask yourself, "Does focusing on all the negative things happening in my life and the world help anyone, including myself? Does it make me happy? Does it attract the kind of people I want in my life? Does it allow me to reintegrate into life? Am I creating the life I want?"

You have choices about your actions. You don't need to act on your feelings or say out loud the things you are thinking. You can choose whether you stay in bed all day, whether to apply for a job, whether to come to work on time, how to act when under stress, how to respond in a relationship.

Step Twelve: Take responsibility for yourself. You have choices.

Think of yourself as your own leader. If you admire someone and want to be like her or him, ask yourself what decisions that person might make and follow her or his example.

I saw a recent TV show on veterans who come home from combat only to join violent motorcycle gangs that fight, rob, and kill. Something in these veterans wouldn't let them stop fighting, couldn't stop their need for excitement and the flow of adrenaline they had become accustomed to during the war. Although I understand their predicament, I also know they had choices. They could have dealt with their addictions to adrenaline, and possibly drugs, in ways other veterans who were recovering from trauma and their addiction. They could have chosen to become involved in activities that were exciting but positive. Instead they *chose* to delve into their dark side. The consequences of their choices were immense.

You too have a choice to make about your life. What kind of a future do you want?

After being emotionally and physically abused by her mother and sexually abused by her stepfather, 15 year old Alexa ran away to Florida and lived on the beach. She got involved with a gang and began to do drugs. Six months later she was arrested for breaking into a house and stealing money and jewelry. She spent several weeks in jail. When I met her, she had been sent home and she was now living in foster care. Shortly after she returned she found out she was pregnant. Thank heaven she lived with a good family who really cared about her. **And she made new choices.** Several years later I received a letter from her letting me know she had completed her Masters degree in business and had started her own business. She was taking good care of her son.

It takes a conscious effort to take responsibility for yourself. You can live responsibly only when you are honest with yourself and look clearly at your feelings, your thoughts, and your actions. Consider how you react during an argument with a family member or friend. Do you run out, get in your car, and screech away at fifty miles per hour? Do you punch the person? Do you retreat and hide in your room and say nothing? Or do you stop, take a minute to think, then consciously choose to go for a walk or write in your journal? Do you rationally assess what is going on inside and what you need to do next? Are you willing to look at yourself instead of automatically blaming other people and circumstances for the situation?

Examine your part in the argument, not just the other person's part. Blaming others won't help *you* solve your problems. As I mentioned earlier, you can't make people change. You can only change yourself. Ask yourself, "What was I doing before the argument occurred? How did I react? Is there something the other person did or said that triggered me emotionally? What may have happened in my past that is similar to what is happening now? Did that memory trigger my anger or my fear? Can I deal with my feelings, or do I need to calm down, then come back, sit down with the person, and talk with him or her in a caring and understanding way when I am ready? If there is something I do (like shaking my finger at people) that causes others to react negatively, will I choose to continue that behavior?" How you act and react, what you decide to do, what you say to yourself and others, is up to you. No one else can make those choices for you.

STEP TWELVE: TAKE RESPONSIBILITY FOR YOURSELF. YOU HAVE CHOICES.

On the other hand, take responsibility only for **your own** actions, not for other people's choices. Sometimes you can influence them for the negative or positive, but ultimately they must be responsible for their own choices, just as you are. You are not in control of others. You are in control only of the things you say to them, the information you give them, and how you act and react. That is your responsibility.

If someone is cruel or uncaring toward you, you have a choice whether to react or to walk away and come back later to talk. What is it about the person's actions that triggers your reaction? Might it be something you don't like in yourself? Or is it a difference of values and beliefs? Don't try to guess what someone else's motives are. Ask.

A couple I counseled were headed for a divorce. Gavin frequently blew up at Jan for not being a responsible person. He said she had lost her job again and he couldn't pay all their bills. He did, however, acknowledge that she was a wonderful mother to their two young children.

Jan admitted she had lost several jobs because she had come to work late, or stayed home when the children were ill, or she felt they needed her. However, she did not agree with Gavin that her actions were irresponsible. As a mother, she believed the needs of her children were more important than her job.

Gavin said that, as a child, his parents had taught him to always be truthful and take responsibility for his actions. If he failed to do a good job, he was severely punished. He hated himself for disappointing his parents whom he said he loved very much. He had tried hard all his life to be responsible.

Now, when he perceived his wife as being irresponsible at work, it triggered him to the point of rage.

By the end of the session, both understood how the other person felt, and they were able to reach a compromise. They agreed to have Jan work part time. What helped them solve their problem? *Honest, nonjudgmental communication.* But remember, to really solve relationship problems, both people will need to be willing to work at making changes.

People act and react according to the information they receive, but sometimes this information can be misread or misperceived. Be sure you have accurate information before you make a decision. Consider the source. For example, if you watch only one TV channel, read one type of newspaper or book, or listen to only one person and believe everything she or he says, your view will be limited. You will act on the one-dimensional snapshot you have created in your mind. Instead, be open to different people's opinions, fully research an issue, talk to people honestly, and ask questions. Look at all sides of an issue before you decide how to act. Humans have a strange way of using information to validate their present belief systems. Think of how many misunderstandings and even wars have started because of missing, partial, or wrong information and perceptions of that information.

However, even if you have reliable information and have researched the problem carefully, you may still make a mistake. Hindsight is great, but you are not clairvoyant. You have limited knowledge in the moment. Don't blame yourself for making a mistake, even though others may. Know that you did the best you could at the time. Sometimes consequences occur in our lives that we cannot predict.

Step Twelve: Take responsibility for yourself. You have choices.

During my career I had many suicidal clients. I would worry about whether I had made the right decisions. None of my clients committed suicide on my watch. I was lucky. Some other very competent psychotherapists were not so fortunate. I knew deep inside that might have been me.

If you made a mistake, or someone else did, you don't need to keep on punishing yourself or others. We are all humans and make mistakes we didn't mean to make, or regret later. Your responsibility is to admit your errors, to learn from them, and, if appropriate, to apologize. Making mistakes is part of life. It is time to forgive yourself and others and move on.

STEP THIRTEEN:
DEAL WITH ALCOHOL AND DRUG ADDICTIONS.

If you have chosen drugs and alcohol as a way to cope with your stress, and they are causing problems in your life, it is time to make a decision about where you wish your life to go. Although I could write pages of suggestions in this area, I won't. First of all, I am not an expert in drug and alcohol abuse counseling, and there are already several excellent books in the area that can be very helpful. Check publishers such as Hazelton and Health Communications on the Internet. Second, I believe that, rather than trying to recover on your own, you will need to join a support group that can help you turn your life around. Recovery deals with much more than stopping doing drugs and/or alcohol.

Although some people have stopped on their own, I suggest you don't set yourself up for failure by going it alone. Drugs and alcohol are so powerful and increase the level of dopamine (pleasure response) so much in your brain that if you are addicted, you will most likely need help to recover. Statistically, addicts make many attempts at sobriety before they succeed. If you really want to change and if you value your spouse, children and loved ones, your own life, or your

Step Thirteen: Deal with Alcohol and Drug Addictions.

job enough that you are truly willing to change rather than lose them, you need to get help.

Here are a few suggestions to help you recover:

1. Join a support group. Tell the people in it that you are going to stop drinking and/or doing drugs. Ask for help. It's not that people have never stopped drugs on their own, but the failure rate is very high. It is easier to continue changes when you are accountable to others and you can call someone when you need support. There are great support groups for addicts. Join a twelve-step program such as Alcoholics Anonymous or Narcotics Anonymous. Choose a sponsor whom you can call day or night if you need to. Also get to know others in the group who will be there for you. The twelve steps are powerful if you work them and they have helped millions. If you don't have a twelve-step program in your area or prefer a different kind of group, veterans can join a VA group or any addicts can join church-based groups for recovering addicts, or community drug programs. If you live in an isolated area, get on the Internet and search to find online recovery groups for drugs and alcohol. Join the one you think matches your needs.

2. Imagine the changes you plan to make, how you will accomplish them, and the rewards you will receive by stopping drinking and doing drugs. Take some quiet time for yourself at least twice a day. Create a new picture in your mind of what your life will be like when you stop drinking or doing drugs. Watch yourself discarding the drugs and alcohol in your house. Watch yourself saying no to friends who encourage you to drink, and see yourself walking away from the situation. See yourself joining a group and talking to some of the people you'll meet there.

See yourself being honest about your addiction. Say out loud to yourself, several times a day, "I am an alcoholic. I am a drug addict." Honestly look at the consequences of your addiction. That will help you break your denial. Now see yourself getting what you want, even to the details of what you look like and what clothes you will be wearing. See how happy your mate is that you are sober. Picture your children running to greet you. See the approval of your boss. Watch yourself getting the job you want. Imagining success will help your brain realize that it is possible and that you can accomplish your goal.

According to research, imagining doing something in great detail is almost as valuable as physically doing it. Olympic athletes such as skiers and swimmers unable to physically practice right before a race frequently use mental imaging to keep up their skills. It works!

3. Start working on changing your thinking and your beliefs. Check Step Seven on changing your thinking. As an alcoholic and drug addict, you have mistaken ideas about life that must be changed before you can fully recover. For example, many addicts think that after a short time they are "cured" and will be able to do drugs or alcohol again. Not true. That's called denial and a sure way to slip back to where you were.

Step Thirteen: Deal with alcohol and drug addictions.

4. Change your behaviors. Check Step Eight on changing unwanted behaviors. Don't punish yourself with reprimands if you make a mistake, but take responsibility for your actions. Only you can change them. Never, never, never give up. Instead, praise and reward yourself every time you succeed, even though that may be only ten percent of the time at the beginning. Remember, habits are hard to break. You don't go from kindergarten to grade twelve in one day. It takes time to develop new pathways in the brain.

5. Call someone from your group and talk before you go out and use. Be honest. Slowly and surely with the help of others, old habits will lessen until the new behavior becomes the "normal one." However, whenever your stress level increases, old habits tend to return. Often they are the first way your mind will tell you to respond. For example, when you lose a job, your first thought may be, "I need a drink," or "I need some meth right now." That's natural. You have used drugs and alcohol, probably for many years, to make you feel better and help you cope. But these thoughts are far from helpful to your recovery. If a situation like that occurs, call someone immediately and talk it through. Find a way to change those thoughts.

6. Avoid places and friends who encourage you to drink or do drugs. Some people think they can return to a bar they used to frequent and keep up old friendships after they stop drinking or using. This is rarely possible. I advise you not to attend functions where large amounts of drugs and alcohol are served. Find a new group of friends who do not use, such as recovering alcoholics and former drug addicts. They understand you and will help you remain sober. If you live in a neighborhood where it isn't possible to avoid old behaviors, you may well need to move. Ask help from the recovery group you are attending.

7. Take it one day at a time. Most recovering addicts will tell you that when it comes to remaining sober, they have to take life one day at a time, sometimes one hour at a time, or one minute at a time. If they can remain sober that day, they can move on to the next day, and the next. Brenda, a former client of mine, told me early on in her recovery that she had promised herself and her husband that she would never drink again. Two months later her children came home to find her passed out on the sofa, a nearly empty bottle of vodka lying beside her. She felt incredible guilt and shame and just wanted to run away.

When it comes to addictions, making long-term promises rarely works. Lower your expectations and keep them realistic. One moment, one day, is all you have. If you use again, start fresh. You deserve a healthy and happy life. Don't give up. You set yourself up for failure if you promise you will never use again.

STEP FOURTEEN:
Use your creativity.

According to recent articles I have read, many psychologists now believe that the best antidote for depression is creativity. Although this is not commonly known, creativity has been found to be a *human need*, just like food and sex. When we are creative, we feel more alive and unique than at any other time. We don't need to be "good at it." We just need to relax and let the creative spirit take us away.

But even knowing these facts, we still delay creative endeavors. Why? We say, "I'm no good at it." Or, "I don't have time." Or, "It's not a priority." But maybe reframing our thoughts will help. "I'm depressed, and being creative will help me get out of this funk." Or, "Creativity is a human need and I need to be creative to feel healthy and whole. It helps me solve my problems."

As the well-known psychoanalyst Carl Jung wrote, "Often the hands know how to solve a riddle with which the intellect has wrestled in vain." During the time Jung left his mentor Freud and diverged from his teachings to develop his own theories, Jung became very depressed and spent hours at the seashore playing in the sand. He created scenes, then destroyed them and rebuilt them in different ways. Gradually his depression and anxiety lifted and he felt clear and whole again. His thinking and his feelings changed, as if by magic.

When you create something you love, you drift into an altered state and time flies. Hours pass before you realize they're gone. New ideas and solutions to problems come into your mind. The unconscious mind finds symbolic answers for your problem without your having to know what is happening inside. You don't need to figure things out consciously.

Creating something, regardless of whatever you decide that something will be, is a form of play and self-expression, and has been present in this world since mankind's early beginnings. Remember the ancient cave art in New Mexico, or the sculptures on Easter Island. Or the Australian aboriginal bark paintings and the Japanese sculpted gardens. Or the ancient peoples who created instruments and wrote and played music. Or designed and created clothes or houses. Or did woodworking. Or developed new food recipes. Or wrote the ancient texts we still read. Or the scientists who have spent years working on new inventions.

Some years ago, my husband and I visited Puerto Vallarta, Mexico. We watched as young men created large sand and rock sculptures on the beach for people to admire and enjoy until the ocean washed them away. Then they would start building again. You could see the intense enjoyment on their faces as they worked. One evening, as we set out for our walk, we noticed a group of men build a brick pathway, and we stopped to admire their work. We were amazed to listen to them discuss and decide on the patterns they would create with the bricks and sand. That pathway became a work of

Step Fourteen: Use your creativity.

art, and we often heard the men laugh and sing as they laid the bricks.

I realized something important on that vacation. Anyone can find ways to be creative, even in her or his daily life and work. It all depends on how people look at something. There are endless ways to be creative, limited only by the imagination.

Here are a few suggestions for you. Use as many of your senses as you can.

1. Create art projects. Art cleanses the soul. Create your own art. You don't have to be what our culture considers a "great" artist. All you need to do is express yourself, your thoughts, your feelings in whatever medium you wish. It can be pencil, colored chalk, paint of any color and kind, and paper. Or it can be wood carving, clay or metal sculpting, or sand and mud. Some people create incredible gardens or sculpt trees and bushes. Art can also be in the form of needle point, knitting, and crocheting. Or weaving and sewing.

Let your mind run wild. You can create forms and scenes of any kind and with any medium you wish. Just let it come out of your hands into your creative endeavors. It is not necessary to have a plan or an image in mind of what you wish to do. What comes out might be as simple as broad brush strokes of dark red and black or quiet greens and blues. Sometimes it is more powerful if you just allow your subconscious brain to do the creating.

Many people have found that it's more fun to work in groups. Examples are woodworking, knitting, and quilting clubs. And recently we have seen the rise of paint and wine groups. What fun! No need to be perfect there.

Several American war veterans' paintings and sculptures, capturing their memories of war now hang in the National Veteran's Art Museum. Russ De Verniero, a talented, award-winning artist and a Vietnam and Panama war veteran, coped with his postwar stress by creating art and music. It became a passion for him and helped him deal with his anger, sleeplessness, and memories. To see his art, check his website: www.seabearartstudio.com. Russ passed away last December from cancer due to agent orange poisoning.

On the other hand it's very important for policemen, firemen, ambulance workers, therapists, and caregivers to cleanse their minds of what they have seen and heard. In order to deal with the horrendous memories he listened to every day while working with American war veterans, Bill Blahd, painted powerful scenes of war and of veterans. His art showing, "In Our Name," is displayed in the gallery of the Linen Building in Boise, Idaho.

2. Photograph the world around you. Photography is another art form. You can take pictures of anything you wish. You can use your smart phone or buy an inexpensive digital camera on eBay or other websites that sell used items. Digital cameras are very forgiving, and you can erase and redo the picture as many times as you wish to get the one you want.

You can photograph a person, an animal, an object, or a scene from diverse perspectives. It will surprise you how differently your favorite tree or car looks from different angles. Not only can you unleash your creativity, but because you

Step Fourteen: Use your creativity.

have to concentrate fully on the scene you wish to take, you will need to keep your mind in the here-and-now.

One man I met who had suffered severe burns in a brush fire and was no longer able to work at the job he had done as a construction worker, felt very lost and depressed. When Kendrick's best friend, a nature photographer, gave him an old camera and asked him to accompany her into the forest to shoot photos, he decided to go, just for something to do. Little did he know that day would change his life. Not only was he able to spend many hours in nature, but he developed a passion for photographing wildlife, especially birds. He has won several awards and sold many of his photos, and is now hired as a photographer for outside weddings and special occasions.

3. Create music. Music is very powerful and important for many people. Create music yourself. Learn to play an instrument that you particularly enjoy and make up your own music. Try different sounds and see what nourishes you. It's fun. You can buy instruments, such as flutes and drums, for very little, or you can make your own. Used guitars are frequently on sale. When I asked a client how she was coping with PTSD, she said she had gone to a drum making workshop and created a drum out of deerskin and wood. Sometimes she spent hours a day in the park close to her house, drumming. It became a daily meditation time for her.

4. Write articles, a book, or poetry. You can write either fiction or nonfiction, although fiction allows you to be more creative. Create a story of anything that comes into your mind. Use your imagination and let it go free. There is no need to judge the story or grammar at this point. Just write. You can write a memoir about events that occurred in your life, or write your autobiography. But if you are writing for creativity and pleasure, focus on the times in your life you enjoyed or that were special to you. It's okay if not every scene is recorded exactly as it occurred. Your memories of the past are not completely accurate at this point, regardless how hard you try to be factual.

5. Do woodworking. The same man who was injured in a brush fire and could no longer work at his construction job remembered how much he had enjoyed woodworking during high school. He built beautiful bunk beds for his two kids out of wood remaining from a neighbor's project, and carved the headboards. His kids loved them, and along with his photography, he felt a purpose and a new focus.

6. Create a garden. For many people, gardening is one of the most engaging and satisfying projects. People who are unable to go out into the wilderness can substitute gardening to help them center and create. Grow a garden or plant some trees, shrubs, and vegetables. Watch them grow. Tend to them. They are a symbol of new life. Move the dirt around and let it sift through your hands. Just placing your hands and/or feet in the earth and moving the dirt is very grounding and centering, as well as calming.

 If you decide to plant a garden, create a plan and prepare the soil before you put out your plants or seeds. Plant the garden the way you wish it to be. You have the power and

Step Fourteen: Use your creativity.

control in your own garden that you may not have in many other parts of your life. You can pull out the weeds, choose any plants you wish, or relocate plants to another area of the garden later if you decide you don't like your first choice. When you nurture the seeds and they begin to grow and change into mature, green, living plants, you will probably feel the same peace and joy you experience out in nature. You water and fertilize the plants and feel you are part of creation.

If you don't live where you can have a garden try growing your plants on your porch in pots or hang them. You can grow vegetables as well as flowers and shrubs. Join a neighborhood garden to grow vegetables for yourself or to give away to soup kitchens and food banks. You are needed.

STEP FIFTEEN:

HAVE FUN. LEARN TO PLAY AGAIN.

ENJOY YOURSELF AND LAUGH.

SOME YEARS AGO A MAN named Norman Cousins wrote a book about his experience of healing from a rare disease. Although the doctors decided they had done everything they could to help him, he was not recovering until he began to watch funny movies and play tapes by comedians who made him laugh. After spending a great deal of his days laughing, he recovered completely. Just as stress changes the body chemistry and reduces the immune system's ability to function, laughter bolsters the immune system to the point where the body, emotions, and mind can often heal.

So have fun, play, and don't judge yourself or others harshly. Being happy is also an emotion, and an incredibly important one to overcome anxiety, sadness, and anger. In order not to get too depressed and anxious, you need to balance the negative emotions with positive ones.

Here are a couple of suggestions:

1. Give yourself permission to be silly, laugh, dance, goof around.

Step Fifteen: Have fun. Learn to play again. Enjoy yourself and laugh.

Learn to play by watching and then joining in with children or with animals. Playgrounds are great fun. Tussle with your kids, mate, and friends. Play games, make snow people, and be a kid again. What did you love to do as a child? Or before your trauma? I spent time this summer watching my grandkids at a playground with their friends. My excuse was that they needed supervision. I listened to them create wild fantasy stories and watched them make up ever changing games. Then they chased each other and the dog. Sometimes I joined in. What I remember most is that I laughed more than I had for a very long time.

Make up stories, swim, dance, do karaoke, play ball, play in the sand at the beach. Just make sure no one gets hurt.

My father, who had PTS most of his life, rarely allowed himself to laugh and to play, and he spent much of his life sullen, anxious, and depressed. He could not let go. Although he was an ethical and religious man and did well financially and physically, his life was not a happy one.

2. Create a sandbox.

This can be used as part of the previous step to be creative but also to have fun and play.

Do you remember how much fun you had in the sand box when you were little? I do. It was just pure creativity and fun! When I was five my father built a sandbox for my sister and me. Sometimes I dumped water into the sand and created mountains, roads, rivers, and villages in it. Then I brought in my toys and I would play for hours at a time, talking to the people and animals, singing and making the sounds of the animals and the cars and trucks. Sometimes I'd create tea parties for my dolls and sometimes I'd take them for a ride. I'd even bring in rocks, twigs and branches with leaves to finish the scene. Other times I'd smash down the sand and create a completely different scene. The nice thing was that no one told me how to do it "right." It was all mine.

One of the techniques I use with people with PTS (children and adults alike) and myself if I have certain issues to resolve or just wish to play, is called sandplay. You can do something similar to help you deal with your trauma as well. Have someone make a wood tray about 20" x 30" x 4" and paint it blue inside to simulate water and sky. Place roughly around 3" of organic sand in it. If you like to add water, a plain plastic tray about the same size is cheap and really easy to find at most department stores.

Then collect small objects such as people, animals, vehicles as well as pinecones, twigs, rocks, moss and anything else that is special to you and you would like to have to create a scene. Find objects you don't like as well as ones you do. Garage sales, bargain stores, and your home are great places to find these objects. Line them up on book shelves and use them to create a scene in the sand whenever you feel down, anxious, or wish to be creative and play. Just doing the play will lift you up. Often it also provides insights to what's going on inside of you, but the play and fun is the most important part for you.

Of course psychotherapists take an extra step to help clients resolve their issues but just the process of the play changes the pathways in the brain, and thus changes the thoughts and feelings. As I mentioned previously, Jung wrote that frequently the hands can solve a problem that the conscious mind cannot.

STEP SIXTEEN:
SPEND TIME IN NATURE.

WE ARE ALL MADE UP of mind, emotion, body, and spirit, and what happens to one of these elements influences and changes the others. Spending time outdoors in nature does not only affect your body; it changes your thoughts and feelings and helps you create a spiritual connection. One of my adolescent clients who had been sexually abused went out into the state park near her foster home every day with her German Shepherd and walked for many miles. She said, "I find peace when I'm out in the wild, and I feel safe, especially with my dog Shep. I wish I could stay forever."

Many veterans and survivors of violence, have moved into the forest. Most of them have been severely stressed by what happened to them. Some men are working for logging companies or the forestry department, and some live far away from their families and civilization in the forest or the mountains, or on the beach. Sometimes they have a dog for companionship, but other than that, they are alone. You may have heard them called homeless, mountain men, beach bums.

Why do people who are severely stressed opt to leave civilization or spend many hours in nature? Most will say they feel at home in nature. Close to God. They feel secure and at peace, less stressed. Everything is quiet. They fish, they hike, they climb, they hunt, they swim, they bike and canoe or ski. Often the experience becomes a meditation.

Interestingly, in sandplay therapy, when I ask people with PTSD to make a scene, they usually create mountains, add rocks, trees, and streams first. Then they stop. When I ask them to add animals, they hesitate, but usually add nonthreatening animals such as dogs, horses, some fish, squirrels, or deer. But when I ask them to add humans, many begin to shake. Some refuse. Why? Because for many people with PTS who have been abused or attacked, humans are threatening.

I don't recommend that you move to the mountains or forest, but I think taking regular breaks to be by yourself in nature, or with someone you trust, is an excellent way to relax and replenish your energy. Go, even if you are handicapped and in a wheelchair. Have a family member or friend take you and stay nearby if you wish to be alone. You will renew your soul. Some of my clients have said to me, "Nature is my church. I feel close to God there."

For those of you who can, take at least one weekend a month and go camping. Fish, hike, canoe, hunt, ski, surf, paint or draw a picture, play an instrument, or just lie under a tree. If you can't go to the forest, go to a park. Get away from people and the humdrum of life. It is essential to replenish your life energy.

Step Sixteen: Spend time in nature.

Growing groups of veterans are turning to outdoor sports to fill in some of what civilian life does not provide. Veterans miss the excitement, camaraderie, and sense of working together as a team. Some veterans act as guides, taking groups out into the wilderness and onto lakes and rivers. Some take out adolescents and Boy Scouts. Most people love being in the outdoors, and it gives them a sense of purpose and comradeship that they no longer have.

Several treatment programs now take groups into the wilderness for a week or longer as a part of therapy. Wikipedia describes "Adventure Therapy" as a therapy that "approaches psychological treatment through experience and action within cooperative games, trust activities, problem-solving initiatives, high adventure, outdoor pursuits, and wilderness expeditions."

Some community services and churches have small groups (both teenagers and adults) that they take out regularly to experience nature. People learn to communicate and connect with each other. They learn to cooperate on projects and trust and rely on each other. Many people say they become so focused and involved in the activities that they almost forget their handicaps and their problems. In the meantime, they also learn new coping skills.

STEP SEVENTEEN:
WORK WITH YOUR PHYSICAL BODY.

---

1. Exercise daily. Exercise helps to rebuild neurons in your brain that are particularly susceptible to stress. There are many forms of exercise, all of which help your brain release endorphins, the brain's "feel good" chemicals. Also, exercise increases muscle tone and reduces levels of stress hormones, like adrenaline and cortisol. After a good workout or bout of physical labor, you will usually feel much more relaxed and happy than you did prior to exercising.

Your body needs at least an hour a day of exercise. Even if other life changes seem overwhelming to you, beginning to exercise more is a simple place to start your recovery. It's not essential to go to a gym, and it is best to increase your exercise slowly if you have not been doing it for a while. As a beginner, don't work out to extremes, nor to the extent that it drives your blood pressure or pulse rate too high. Run down your street or along the beach, climb a tree, lift jugs of sand, throw balls with your kids or with a couple of friends, build a tree house, cultivate your garden, dance. Only your imagination can limit you.

Many gyms offer instruction in the martial arts. Not only are the martial arts a great way to exercise, but they

Step Seventeen: Work with your Physical Body.

also teach discipline and encourage you to feel strong and powerful again. Maybe you have been threatened or attacked in the past and you felt you had no control. The martial arts give you the confidence to break out of your fears and isolation. When I worked in Baltimore I saw several clients who had been raped and one of the first things I advised them to do is to learn some form of martial arts.

Yoga is another form of structured exercise that includes meditation and discipline. If yoga classes are offered in your area, check them out.

2. Get enough sleep. Many people with PTS have difficulty sleeping. Most doctors now say that these people don't have a sleep disorder, but rather a hyper-arousal disorder, where their brains release stress hormones such as adrenaline and cortisol into the blood and won't let them relax. Over time these increased stress hormones can actually change the brain patterns.

Why might you be over-aroused? You have probably spent many hours on alert, always waiting, watching even after the event that created your trauma. People with Complex PTSD never felt safe. You felt that if you were not ready to act at a moment's notice, you or someone you loved might be hurt or die. Your mind told you over and over again to be constantly watchful, vigilant, prepared. So now you can't relax enough to fall asleep. This learned brain pattern of hyper-arousal doesn't change suddenly even when you are safe. Your unconscious mind continues to tell you that you must be on alert.

For most people, sleep deprivation has very negative effects on the body, especially the brain. People often say that they feel they are "going crazy" when they have insomnia. They cannot deal with even minimal stress. Small problems may send them into rages, or they may fall apart emotionally, shaking and crying. And the longer they go without sleep, the worse their problems become. Survivors may develop high blood pressure or diabetes, or become obese. The immune system doesn't work as well as it should and they get sick more often.

How can you begin to sleep again? Your brain will need to be retrained. You will have to learn to trust again and believe that you are safe. Changing these thinking processes takes time, so don't get discouraged. Sleep and reduced arousal are essential to health and well-being. Please see a therapist and a doctor as soon as possible for advice and/or medication.

Here are a few ideas you can try to help you sleep at night. Experiment to find the ones that work best for you.

- At least an hour before you plan to go to sleep, stop watching, reading, and doing things that excite you or that create anxiety. Change your thinking to something that helps you relax and feel secure. Watch a funny movie, read a self-help or inspirational book, listen to a relaxation CD. What you do might even be boring. My "drug of choice" is history. All I need to do is to read a chapter in a history book with all the dates and facts, and I am sound asleep.
- Find out what helps *you* relax. This may be different for each person. When your body relaxes, your

Step Seventeen: Work with your physical body.

anxiety and hyper-arousal decrease. Your blood pressure and pulse rate fall. A few things that help people relax are a warm glass of milk, a cup of tea, a funny movie, relaxing music, relaxation tapes (e.g., Louise Hay CDs), hypnosis tapes, a warm shower or hot bath, and deep breathing and relaxation exercises (See Step Four for suggestions.)

- Keep your room cool (60-65 degrees F). Take a cool shower or open your window to allow the cool air to flow over your body.
- Remember times you slept well and imitate that feeling. Breathe in and out, slowly and deeply. Ask yourself where you felt safe before the trauma, perhaps in your childhood bedroom or in the forest. If you don't feel safe at that place anymore, where do you feel safe now? Then imagine yourself there, completely safe and relaxed. Look all around and explore the environment: what do you see, hear, smell? Relax each set of muscles from the toes to the head. Or imagine yourself floating in space, on a cloud, or down a river toward peaceful, safe sleep. Allow yourself to drift.
- Use mindfulness meditation.
- Practice safe touching and relaxation. Although many people seem to be hesitant to touch others, touch is a very important part of human life from the moment we are born to the moment of death. Safe touching is reassuring, respectful, and loving. Ask the receiver for permission to touch or hug them. Gently touching and hugging a partner, your children, your

family, and your friends helps you connect and bond to each other.

Yes, touching can make you feel more vulnerable, but it can also help you relax and feel safe, supported, and cared for. Snuggle in bed with your partner, or hold each other. Hold your children and let them sit on your lap. Hug a friend or relative. Safe touching cannot be faked. It must be sincere and heartfelt.

If you feel too uncomfortable just holding your partner in your arms, give each other a massage. This is a great way to meet each other's touching needs. Have your partner give you a massage on a weekly basis and exchange massages with her or him. Explore with each other. Learn how to do this in books, a class, or on the Internet. If you do not have a mate, find out if there is a massage school nearby where you can get a therapeutic massage for less cost. Get some kind of bodywork weekly if possible, especially deep body massage, to help you relax.

- Reduce UVB light before bed. Avoid screen time at least an hour before bed. This includes computers, television, and your Smartphone.
- Ensure exposure to daytime light. Use a Light Box for an hour in the winter if you live in an area where you have little sunlight.
- Use "tapping", or as it is formally called, the Emotional Freedom Technique (EFT). It is often considered to be the emotional version of acupuncture, but without the needles. EFT interrupts the emotional cycle in your body and calms the nervous system, thereby

Step Seventeen: Work with Your Physical Body.

reducing your state of hyper-arousal. It helps you rebalance your energy enough to relax and fall asleep. See Step Twenty for more information about EFT and other innovative techniques.

- Change your thinking by reminding yourself that you are safe now and you are home (see Step Seven). Stop continuously running negative or worry thoughts through your mind, and learn to trust again. Think of the positive things in your life. Repeat a mantra that helps you relax and trust, e.g., "I trust God (or substitute another word of your choice) to provide for me." You can also read quieting and positive materials to help shut down your negative thoughts. Do something non-stimulating that does not require a lot of energy from your brain, and it will slow down.
- Journal and "dump" your problems. Many people, both men and women, write their thoughts and emotions in a journal before they go to bed. Journaling helps them let go of their worries enough to fall asleep. To assure that you feel safe enough to write whatever comes into your mind, keep your journal somewhere no one can find it. A small safe or a locked drawer works well.
- As mentioned earlier, exercise or work out physically during the day but not within 3 hours of bedtime. If you can, take up a job or hobby during the day that exhausts you physically.
- Don't smoke, drink coffee or anything containing caffeine for at least four hours before bedtime. Instead, drink or eat something containing tryptophan (helps

induce sleep) like turkey or warm milk. Don't eat 3 hours before bedtime.
- Consider taking a vitamin, herb, or over-the-counter drug. The following are some that have been shown to help: Magnesium Glycinate, Vitamin D3, L-tryptophan and 5-HTP, Theanine, Melatonin, Valerian root, GABA, and certain antihistamines like Benadryl. Some essential oils also work. Consult an herbalist or natural food store to find out more before trying them.
- Don't take naps during the day. Researchers have found that many people take naps during the day and then can't sleep at night.

Ted, a former policeman who had been shot during a drug raid, told me reluctantly that he couldn't sleep at night, but he could sleep during the day. So he slept much of the day while his wife was at work, and then stationed himself in his wheelchair at the front door on full alert at night. He kept his gun on his lap. With long-term therapy, medication, and the help of his wife, Ted eventually stopped taking naps and relaxed enough at night to turn his sleep patterns around.

But some people with PTS can sleep neither during the day nor at night. If that is you, try lying down on the sofa for a bit and relaxing during the day. Tell yourself you are safe now, and it's okay to fall asleep. No one will harm you. Over time you will begin to nap for brief periods. That's okay. Nap for a while. Let your body and your mind remember what it is like to sleep, and that it is safe to do so now.

Step Seventeen: Work with your physical body.

One of my clients, Julie, survived by hanging onto a branch when her canoe overturned on a swift river. She was terrified she would lose consciousness and let go of the branch. Although Julie was not aware how long it took, she was finally rescued by helicopter.

After the accident she was unable to fall asleep. She spent hours roaming around in her house. She tried reading, listening to music, and watching TV, but her hyper-alert mind would not allow her to sleep. At night she would doze for just a moment, then suddenly jerk awake, afraid she was back on the river and she would let go of the branch and drown. Her body shook, her heart raced, and she wanted to scream.

After a month of not sleeping, she finally went to see her doctor who prescribed sleeping medication and anxiety-reducing drugs, and suggested she see a psychotherapist. She came to me shortly after. The drugs and counseling worked, and she was eventually able to sleep several hours a night, but still could not fall asleep on her own. After a while she began to sleep naturally for about half an hour, but only during the day. Sometimes she would still jerk awake with nightmares. But she was thrilled to know that she could fall asleep on her own. She had felt it would never happen. Over the months she began to sleep peacefully for an hour during the day, and slowly she started sleeping at night. By the time I stopped seeing her, she was still using sleeping medication, but only as needed.

- Work with your nightmares. At first you may have nightmares when you fall asleep. That's because your brain is still hyper-alert and overactive. Just keep repeating the words before you go to sleep and when you wake up, "It's okay. Dreams are not real, and I am safe." Let yourself shake after the dream (see Step Twenty). As you begin to relax more, and work through your trauma experience, the nightmares will lessen. If you are working with a psychotherapist you might want to look into your dreams more fully.

3. Eat a healthy diet with conscious intention.
Over the many years that the human body has evolved, nature has determined what will keep your body and mind healthy and working to its maximum potential. What you eat and drink will nurture you or harm you. Your body will eventually succumb to diseases if you put foods, drink, and chemicals into it that nature did not mean to be there. That includes alcohol, drugs, cigarettes, and poisons such as insecticides and herbicides.

Stress increases cortisol in the bloodstream. Research has linked this higher level of cortisol to lowered immunity and heightened depression and blood sugar-related diseases, such as obesity and diabetes. So you will need, even more than others, a nourishing diet to keep your immune system and cells healthy, and the chemicals in your body and mind balanced. When you eat healthy meals you will find you have more energy and reduced anxiety, and your blood sugar levels and blood pressure will often stabilize.

Step Seventeen: Work with your physical body.

So what is a healthy balanced diet? There is no single answer. For each person it will be somewhat different. But here are a few general rules:

- As you learned in school, your diet should include fruits, vegetables (especially green vegetables), some whole grains, proteins such as nuts, beans, meat, fish, cheese, milk, and eggs, plus essential oils such as fish oils, certain vegetable oils, and nut oils.
- Limit refined carbohydrates such as white breads, pastries, soft drinks, and sugar of any kind. Refined carbohydrates seem to keep cortisol levels high in your bloodstream. Sugar is processed much like alcohol in the body and can create rapid mood changes and fatigue. Although sugary foods are comforting and can seem to reduce stress, they actually raise your stress hormone levels.
- If possible, eat fresh, whole, natural, and preferably organic foods. These are more expensive than processed foods but, in the long run, will keep you healthier, so you will spend less on healthcare.
- If you don't eat a healthy diet and are under stress, it is important to add a good multivitamin. Vitamin B complex, Vitamin C, Vitamin D, and magnesium are among the first vitamins to be depleted in times of stress.

I realize that when you are under a lot of stress, it is easy to relapse into either not eating enough, or "comfort eating" and eating too much. The extra stress of shopping for healthy foods and preparing them may be more than you think you can handle. You want your life to be as simple as possible. But there are consequences to choosing the easy way out.

When I met Sally, a survivor of sexual abuse who had PTSD, she had recently been divorced. She lived alone in a small apartment and worked for a fast food diner. By the time she got off work, she felt exhausted and jittery. The last thing she wanted to do was cook for herself, so each day she brought home pizza or a hamburger and fries, and washed it all down with a large soft drink.

At home she felt lonely, anxious, and depressed. To help herself feel better, she ate doughnuts and drank soft drinks while watching TV. In the morning she ate a couple of more doughnuts and drank three cups of coffee. Usually she skipped lunch.

After several months Sally had gained a considerable amount of weight, but what concerned her even more was that she experienced constant fatigue and frequent chest pains. When she finally saw her doctor her blood pressure, cholesterol, and blood sugar levels were high. Fortunately the dire warning of her doctor shocked her enough to take action. With the help of a nutritionist, she changed her diet. She joined Weight Watchers and decided to adopt a dog at the local shelter. She started running with her dog daily.

Stress eating: The problem with stress eating is that it often becomes a habit that later is hard to break. As soon as your stress increases, you either

Step Seventeen: Work with your physical body.

eat less and less or turn to food for comfort. Some people develop bulimia. You may crave certain foods you love. Strict diets may work for short periods, but you will tend to return to your old eating habits when your motivation diminishes or stress increases.

Eating disorders with people who have PTS are common and are very difficult to resolve on your own. They are often considered to be addictions and thus need help from a psychotherapist and/or a group such as a 12 Step program.

Here are a few tips to help you change your stress eating habits:

- Use the previous steps in this book to reduce your stress level. With reduced stress, stress-related eating usually normalizes. If it doesn't seek help.
- Change the way you look at yourself and food. Body image and weight can motivate you to diet, but the motivation usually doesn't last, and thoughts of food become obsessive and take up far too much space in your mind. It is more lasting to change your thinking about yourself and the food you eat. You may need to stay away from the mirror. Some people have a completely distorted image of themselves. They may think they are fat even when they are much too thin.
- Make your motivator good health. Learn to love, appreciate, and accept yourself. Tell yourself that you deserve and want to be healthy. Imagine yourself healthy and happy, doing what you like to do. Place a

picture of yourself when you were healthy where you can see it frequently every day.

- Think before you put something into your body and make a conscious decision to eat. Are you actually hungry? Will this particular food nourish you or hurt you? If you tend to be the kind of person who reduces food input dramatically under stress, make conscious decisions about your food. Even if you don't feel like eating, pick up some nutritious foods on your way home. Eat the food slowly and in small amounts, several times a day.
- It's okay to have something like ice cream or your favorite food once a day so you don't feel deprived and punished.
- Put notes on your bathroom mirror, in your car, in your bedroom, reminding yourself of your new way of thinking, and read them several times a day.
- Try conscious eating. I challenge you to try something new. Most of the time we are barely aware of what we put into our bodies. We hurry through our day and think about what we need to do next. We eat to live or eat to reduce stress. But what if we took the time and energy to become fully aware of our food and learned to enjoy every bite we ate, appreciating it in the moment? What if we became purposefully attentive to the here and now, using all our senses and noting what we experienced as we ate, and how we responded to our food? How would our body respond? Maybe it would integrate the food more fully

Step Seventeen: Work with your physical body.

and use all the nutrients in it to keep us healthier. Here are a few tips to help you try this new approach:

    a. Read Step Five on self-awareness and mindfulness.

    b. Eat at least one meal a day at a place where you feel most comfortable, and where you will have no distractions such as the TV or the Internet. At work you might find a place where you can be alone and relax.

    c. Take each bite and chew it slowly.

    d. Instead of allowing your mind to wander, especially to worries, stay in the present and concentrate on your food.

    e. Use all your senses. What does the food look like, taste like, smell like and feel like in your mouth? Enjoy the flavor of the food.

In the long run, what you eat and drink is ultimately your choice. No one else can make those decisions for you. However, remember to stay conscious in the process and make whatever you decide to put into your body a true choice.

STEP EIGHTEEN:
REBUILD YOUR PURPOSE IN LIFE. VOLUNTEER YOUR TIME OR LOOK INTO GETTING A MEANINGFUL JOB.

As mentioned earlier, PTS survivors often say that life no longer has meaning for them. They feel lost and without purpose. Feeling as if they have no purpose leads to emptiness, stress, and depression. They feel helpless and as if they have no control over their own lives, much less the world around them. When I talked to Mary, a nurse and the survivor of a brutal attack on her way home from the hospital, it was obvious she was becoming increasingly depressed as her court date came nearer. She was afraid the defense lawyer would "tear her apart" and she knew she couldn't handle it at this point. I asked her, "Have you been thinking of suicide?"

She shrugged, then said, "Why should I be here? I have no purpose anymore. I go to work every day but my job now has no meaning. Nobody cares whether I am here. I have not been out with my friends for a long time and I'm going to be all alone when I go to court. I'm scared I'm going to fall apart and land up on the psychiatric ward. And then what?"

I asked, "How did you feel before the trauma?"

Step Eighteen: Rebuild your purpose in life.

Her eyes brightened and she straightened her shoulders. "I spent time talking to my patients but most important, I spent time taking care of and playing with my sister's kids after work. What I did made a big difference in my nieces lives. We had lots of fun playing together and I'd teach them things. They adored me and I adored them." Her voice rose with excitement as she talked about the children. When she finished, she had tears in her eyes.

I said, "I noticed the change in your face and your body when you told me about playing with your sister's children. What was happening inside of you?"

She leaned back and nodded. "Okay. I see what you mean. I need to be out there doing things with others. To have fun. Especially with kids. That's what gives my life meaning."

"Is there a reason you stopped seeing the children?" I said.

She hung her head. "They're gone. They moved just before... you know. The trauma." She swallowed hard.

"Is there anything you can think of that you could do with children or that you feel is important? It could be for money but it could also be as a volunteer."

We spent some time listing some of the things she could look into and a week later she came back saying she was volunteering at a daycare for disadvantaged children on her days off. She had also asked the supervisor at the hospital to transfer her to a children's ward.

I suggest you take the time to be with others and help those who have gone through something similar to your experience. Or like Sally, work with disadvantaged children. Your service could be to anyone who has experienced stress after a trauma or anyone who needs your love and support. In helping others, you may find healing for yourself.

Remember, you have unique and vital skills and gifts to give other people. Ask yourself what skills or abilities you learned in your life both as a child and adult that you can use with others. If you have difficulty thinking of them ask friends and family members for suggestions as well, and write them down. Remember that your trauma experience has given you special insight and compassion with other people who have gone or are going through a trauma.

Here are some ideas to help you discover a new purpose. Some of these are paid jobs and some are not. But what do you have to lose, especially if you're not working at this point? Volunteering may even help you develop skills that will be useful in a job search later on. Remember, whether you are a woman or a man you are needed in all these situations.

1. **Rescue.** If you are still young and healthy you can work in the police force or join the FBI, but also consider becoming a firefighter or emergency medical technician (EMT). One of my friends, Patsy, spent this last summer fighting fires. For anyone who needs a purpose and is strong and healthy, more and more, as the climate changes, countries are facing emergencies such as the Haiti earthquake, Hurricane Katrina, and Super-storm Sandy. Hurricanes, tornados, and floods leave towns devastated. Fires burn miles and miles of forests and homes. Everywhere we look, it seems, people need to be rescued, fed, and housed. Even if you can't actually do the hard work you can cook, organize teams, or make calls.

STEP EIGHTEEN: REBUILD YOUR PURPOSE IN LIFE.

2. **Rebuild.** As big cities like Detroit are going bankrupt, buildings and infrastructures are disintegrating. Families, youth, and neighborhoods need help and support to rebuild. Habitat for Humanity builds housing for those who can't afford to build their own. Cities and counties need help rebuilding infrastructure such as roads, sewer lines, and water lines.

3. **Feed the hungry.** People are hungry and food prices have risen precipitously. Both the homeless and low income people need your help. You can help collect and distribute food for the hungry. Or work in soup kitchens. In some locales, people are banding together to find or create a space where they can recycle their organic waste into the soil and grow their own food locally. If you enjoy gardening and working with your hands, helping out in these projects will be satisfying (and you'll often get some great free food as well).

4. **Teach the young.** Our youth today are floundering and need to receive love but also learn discipline to know someone cares. Join a community or church youth project, the Scouts, or Big Brothers/Big Sisters, or babysit to give hope to a child. You can be an incredible example and role model for our young people. A longitudinal research study conducted some time ago in Hawaii indicated that those children that had grown up in poverty but had had at least one loving mentor that believed in them and they identified with closely, were the children who became most successful when they grew up.

5. **Help someone like yourself.** Even if you are disabled in some way, help your fellow PTS survivors who are physically or emotionally damaged and you will help yourself as well. Join groups or create groups in your community or online. Give talks or write blogs for websites. Write articles for newspapers, or letters to the editor. Work in crisis centers and on hotlines to help others deal with their problems and emergencies. Or just go talk to a lonely neighbor.

Pat, a Vietnam veteran, recently spoke for the first time of his war experiences and recovery from PTSD. He gave his talk to a large group of veterans and civilians on Memorial Day. As he watched the crowd, he could see that they were visibly moved by what he said. At the end of his talk, they stood up and cheered. Several recent veterans came up to him afterward to talk and ask questions. Later, Pat said that he finally felt supported by the people of America after being called a "baby killer" when he came home. He was able to release his shame and guilt of having served in Vietnam and felt he could move on.

Helen who had been sexually abused as a child by her neighbor had been threatened with her life and she told no one for many years. Then finally she told her family and friends what had happened to her. They were shocked and grieved with her. When she worked with me she wrote her story and gave it to me to share with other clients. Over time I collected about 20 stories of trauma and recovery from clients who wanted me to share their experiences to help others in similar situations and give them hope of recovery. That booklet helped many.

STEP EIGHTEEN: REBUILD YOUR PURPOSE IN LIFE.

6. **Influence public policy.** Contact your legislators or city council and work with them to help create jobs, better health care, and better living conditions for everyone here at home.

STEP NINETEEN:

Explore new technologies.

MANY OF THE NEW TECHNOLOGIES alter brain waves. Neuroscientists are now finding that recovery from PTSD is much faster if they can use electrical and magnetic brain stimulation to reset the brain wave patterns that have been disrupted by trauma. The goal is to return the brain patterns to normal. Remember, when severe trauma (fight or flight) occurs, the amygdala (emotional brain) becomes hyperactive and won't stop triggering, and the hippocampus (time and long term memory brain) and the prefrontal cortex (logical thinking brain) become underactive in people with PTSD.

Here are a few new technologies and devices that are being researched and are promising:

1. Deep Brain Stimulation: This is a technique used for people who have PTSD that is resistant to other treatment. At present research is indicating there is a specific area in the amygdala (emotional brain) called the basolateral nucleus that is hyperactive in people who have PTSD. There is

Step Nineteen: Explore new technologies.

a correlation between increased activity among brain circuits and flashbacks.

Intracranial electrodes are placed into this area and an electrical signal is sent through an electrode into the brain to reset the brain waves to normal. The same technique can be used to deliver stimuli to other specific areas in the brain. It has been shown to work for resistant depression as well as Parkinson's and other neurological disorders. However, it is invasive and must be done as a surgical procedure.

2. Brain Stimulation Patch: A special patch is placed on the forehead while the person sleeps. It changes the brain wave patterns and reduces PTSD symptoms. The advantage is that it is not invasive and can be removed or changed at any time.

3. Transcranial Magnetic Stimulation Devices: These modulate the prefrontal cortex which is underactive in people who have PTSD, and increase the cortex activity.

4. Electric Shock Treatment (ECT): Although used in the past for resistant depression it is not used much anymore. It does, however, stimulate the brain waves to reset and under certain circumstances is still utilized.

5. Neurobiofeedback : It has been found to be very useful in resetting the brain waves back to normal. Some psychotherapists around you may well be using this machine for PTSD. Call around and find out.

6. Reset Therapy: A neuropsychologist, Dr. George Lindenfelt, developed a noninvasive technique that he finds rapidly decreases the PTSD memories and resets the core trauma circuits in the brain. He uses a headset and sends binaural resonant frequency beats into the ears while the client recalls the trauma memory. Each ear hears something different. It is considered to be a neuro-acoustical intervention that reconsolidates the memories. According to Dr. Lindenfelt the changes last.

7. Stellate Ganglion Block: An ordinary anesthetic is injected into the stellate ganglion (nerve tissues) in the neck to stop pain but according to researcher Dr. Eugene Lipov it also decreases the fight, flight symptoms in PTSD. His clients rave about the results. Although the research so far has not been duplicated, the research is continuing. You might want to keep an eye on this one.

8. Technologies for veterans: Next I will mention some other devices specifically researched and created for veterans. The military is actively financing researchers (6.7 million dollars) to find ways to help veterans with PTSD. But the therapies will be just as useful in the future for anyone who is a trauma survivor.

a) Simulation Exposure Therapy: In 2005, Albert Rizzo, a professor of psychiatry at the University of Southern California, received a grant from the military to modify video games in order to help veterans returning from Iraq and Afghanistan cope with PTSD. Rizzo found that by immersing veterans in re-creations of combat, they could

Step Nineteen: Explore new technologies.

overcome the devastating patterns of avoiding anything that would remind them of their traumas. He adapted virtual reality, as we know it, into "Simulation Exposure Therapy" for service people. It is a type of technology that recreates virtual environments similar to those of the trauma using stories, realistic characters, and special effects to trigger the sights, sounds, and even vibrations and smells of combat, such as gunfire and smoke. Working with a trained therapist, the veteran undergoing Simulation Exposure Therapy wears 3-D glasses to make the experience as realistic as possible. It is used together with slow and methodical therapy.

Simulation Exposure Therapy gives therapists a way to take people back through the trauma that has triggered PTS, in order to help them overcome their symptoms. In a small study of twenty veterans who completed eleven Simulation Exposure Therapy sessions, sixteen no longer met the criteria for PTSD after treatment. At present Dr. Barbara Rothbaum of the Department of Psychiatry at Emory University is treating veterans with exposure therapy using virtual reality plus D-Cycloserine, an antibiotic that reduces adrenaline. The treatment looks promising.

In a book called *At War with PTSD*, Dr. Robert McLay discusses what he calls, "facing the ghosts of war in a computer simulator." He claims that simulators have been used experimentally on the front lines since 2008 to immediately address PTSD reactions and reduce the risk. Although it appears that the sooner a person can face the trauma after it happens, the less likely PTSD or PTS will occur, this technique is still considered experimental.

b) SimCoach: While psychiatrists like Dr. Rizzo are using realistic video games to help veterans overcome their reluctance to seek help for emotional problems, visiting a clinic can still carry a stigma about being seen as weak for seeking help. For those who prefer taking a more private approach, SimCoach is a "virtual mental health guide" on the Internet that keeps all information completely anonymous, without the need to visit a clinic. With SimCoach, the virtual coach asks questions about your symptoms. When you type in your responses, SimCoach then guides you to appropriate advice and resources. According to the developers, SimCoach is not connected to the military, and that if you are a family member or loved one afraid of breaking the confidentiality of a veteran, this is a safe place to get answers.

Visit www.simcoach.org or www.braveheartveterans.org/SimCoach to meet "Virtual Vietnam Veteran Bill," a virtual character who has suffered from PTSD. While he can't diagnose your symptoms, he can give you a lot of information.

c) SimSensei: A newer version of the SimCoach technology SimSensei should be available in military bases and VA hospitals. This latest version actually senses and interprets muscle movement in the body (body language), emotional states, vocal patterns. and hand gestures to better guide the computer responses and give the veteran more realistic, targeted feedback.

STEP TWENTY:
Try these special techniques.

SEVERAL TECHNIQUES HAVE BEEN SHOWN to be helpful for people with severe PTS, such as biofeedback, hyperbaric oxygen treatment, and Amygdala Retraining (developed by Ashok Gupta). The following are a few I have used personally and with clients, and know to be effective in reducing symptoms of PTS. They are best learned with the help of a professional versed in the area. But both "tapping" and "shaking" are techniques you can continue doing on your own whenever you need them, once you have learned them.

1. Eye Movement Desensitization Reprocessing (EMDR)
Extensive research studies have shown that Eye Movement Desensitization and Reprocessing (EMDR) is at present the most powerful and rapid technique used by psychotherapists to deal with disturbing memories of post trauma stress, panic attacks, trouble sleeping, depression, anger, and anxiety. It can bring quick and lasting relief for many kinds of emotional problems.

EMDR is a therapeutic process using right/left eye movements or bilateral physical stimulation that repeatedly activates the opposite sides of the brain. This process releases trauma memories, emotions, and negative thoughts that are caught in the nervous system, allowing people to "integrate," or create a connection between the "feelings and images" part of the brain and the logical "thinking" brain, where words and meaning reside. Many psychotherapists dealing with trauma will be well versed in the procedure.

During EMDR, the therapist will move her/his finger back and forth in front of your face. At the same time, s/he will ask you to remember your feelings and memories about your traumatic experience, or a present-day event that triggered an intense reaction. You will closely track the movement of the finger, back and forth, as though watching a ping-pong ball, while recalling memories, thoughts, and feelings.

Ideally this process will help resolve the issues and rapidly decrease the negative feelings. It is most effective when used in conjunction with other techniques, such as Cognitive Behavioral Therapy (see Step Seven), ordinarily used by psychotherapists to desensitize you to your trauma. Techniques such as prolonged contact with your trauma environment, either by imagining it or actually confronting it are also frequently used along with EMDR.

2. Emotional Freedom Technique (EFT), or "Tapping"

Many of you may have heard of "tapping," and, like I, may have rolled your eyes in disbelief. Tapping different parts of your head and body while saying something? Really? But actually the technique is proving to be very effective for stress-sufferers, especially people with PTS or PTSD. Dawson Church, Ph.D., recently has conducted a number of clinical trials of EFT, the latest ones focusing on Iraq

Step Twenty: Try these special techniques.

veterans who have been diagnosed with PTSD. Testing stress hormone levels before and after EFT, Dr. Church has found a considerably lowered cortisol level after EFT. Depression and anxiety are reduced.

If you decide to try it, you will need to recall the issue and the specific trauma memory as you tap on different body meridians with your fingertips, and repeat a specific affirmation which ends in, "I deeply love and accept myself." Although I will not mention here exactly where you need to tap or what you need to say, there are great sites online that will lead you through a tapping session so that if you are unable to find a therapist who uses EFT, or are out in a rural area, you can learn it via the Internet. Some helpful sites are listed at the end of this section.

Some people call EFT the emotional version of acupuncture, but without the needles. Like acupuncture, EFT affects the body's subtle energy system and meridians. Others believe that, similar to EMDR, tapping interrupts a person's emotional cycle by confusing the brain. It tells the body to "stand down" while the brain releases the emotions and calms the nervous system, thus reducing the body's state of hyper-arousal, and increases the rebalancing energy.

EFT practitioners believe that the cause of all negative emotions is a disruption in the body's energy system, and that trauma is retained at a cellular level. Regardless of when your trauma occurred, the data is still stored inside your cells, and the memory is trying to protect your body from being traumatized again. EFT helps you clear these cells and return them to normal.

There are several amazing stories online of people recovering from PTSD with the help of EFT. A Vietnam veteran whom I know personally had suffered from severe PTSD since his war experience forty years ago. He had been in therapy for years and had used several drugs for anxiety, nightmares, flashbacks, and inability to sleep, until a year ago, when he finally consulted a therapist who used EFT. Although, like all survivors with PTSD, he longed to be free from his pain, he had little faith in the technique itself. He told me that he had tried too many "cures" to believe any would actually work. But EFT did work. Now he taps daily, and sometimes many times a day, when he begins to feel anxious. At present he is off all medications and enjoys what he calls a "normal" life.

Tapping, like other techniques, can be learned on your own, but for maximum effectiveness, you should learn it from a practitioner who specializes in the technique.

Here are some websites I have found helpful. All teach you how to use EFT:

tryitoneverything.com
emofree.com (the site of Gary Craig, founder of EFT)
thetappingsolution.com by Nick Ortner.

3. Tension and Trauma Release Exercises (TREs), or "Shaking"
As I mentioned earlier, shaking is one of the body's natural responses to trauma or severe fright. Animals do it, children do it, and adults do it. However, many of us have grown up thinking that to show fear is to acknowledge we are weak, so we do our best to stop our bodies from doing what they

Step Twenty: Try these special techniques.

would naturally do to release the energy from the trauma. We hold the stress inside our bodies and muscles, where it creates pain, emotional tension, and illness.

Of course, at times you are not able to stop and take the time to shake, so tension remains stored in the body, to be released in the future. But in most situations you will probably not take the time to shake on purpose later, when you are alone and relaxed. When the discharge of energy doesn't occur, the brain translates this tension into intense emotions such as rage and shame.

Several years ago, after experiencing a severe trauma, I found my body automatically jerking and wanting to shake whenever I started to relax. At first I restrained my body. But then I realized that if I gave my body permission to jerk and shake for a while, I felt relieved and much less stressed. So I started to shake for about twenty minutes a day before I went to bed. I was amazed at the difference it made in the way I felt, both emotionally and physically.

Dr. David Berceli first developed a specific shaking technique to release stress and trauma from the body while working with people immediately or shortly after natural disasters and political violence in various countries. These tension and trauma release exercises have been shown to be very effective with military personnel as well. At present these special techniques are taught in workshops or by therapists all over the country and in several areas of the world.

If you don't have access to learning this technique, lie down on your back on the floor. Take several deep breaths and then imagine seeing a dog shake after a trauma. Give your body permission to shake,, understanding that it's a normal process that our bodies have developed over a very long time to release excess energy after a frightening experience. If it feels uncomfortable for you to shake in front of others, do the shaking in private.

Check http://tensionprevention.com for information.

Conclusion

And so we come to the end of the steps of the ladder to recovery and resilience. I sincerely hope this book has helped you on your journey to a more fulfilling life. No one can conclude this book better than Patrick Overton, the Vietnam veteran who wrote in his poem:

The Healing Wall, Part IV

IV.
I left the Wall
I ascended from the deep hole.
Tired, emotionally exhausted,
I looked back where I had been.
I knew my pain had not magically left me
I carry it with me today
But I carry it, it no longer carries me.
This was the healing I could not find before
The Wall told me my name was not there
*and said, "**Go live your life, you do not belong here,**"*
And so I do, live my life now, beyond the Wall.

And this I wish for you: that **you** may carry your pain instead of **it** carrying you. And so go on and live your life now beyond the trauma you have experienced.

PART 3

FAMILIES AND FRIENDS

Widow's Song

He did not come back,
That scarred half-man
In a wheelchair who stares
At nightmares I cannot see
And, asleep, screams in the night.

by Linda Farrell Erickson

A Path Beyond Post Traumatic Stress

Illusion

Stalks of wheat bend in the August wind,
Lean toward a taut barbed wire fence,
Welcome the structure of containment,
On a prairie with miles of open space.

A small child flattens the stems of grain,
Smoothes a hand knit sweater for her head,
Nestles into the tiny home,
And blends into the ripening wheat field.

She hears the wheat rustle in the wind,
Hears the robin chirp, chirp overhead,
Forgets the screams of her sister
And the crack of mama's whip on her back.

by Anna Goodwin

Introduction to Families and Friends

While I was working as a therapist, and also while I was writing this book, I talked to many family members and close friends of survivors of trauma. Invariably they asked me how they could help their loved ones. Recently I met with a friend who had married a Vietnam veteran while he was in the midst of his war trauma. He had been diagnosed with PTSD about eight years after the war.

I knew that both partners had years of therapy, together and alone, and were now doing well in the relationship, so I asked Rachel how their marriage had survived all these years.

She looked at me, sighed, and said, "Patience, unlimited patience."

We talked for a while and then she said, "You know, I had to learn to not take what he said or did personally, or I'd be hooked into an argument that fast." She snapped her fingers.

I asked her what she thought was her husband's major issue during those years.

"Control," she said immediately. "Major control issues. When he felt he wasn't in control, he would go crazy. He'd yell and throw things."

A Path Beyond Post Traumatic Stress

Before we parted I asked her what she had learned in all these years and whether I could include some of her story in this book.

"Yes of course. Tell the families it's really hard at times to live with someone who has PTSD, and I think they need to get all the help they can. But the good thing about sticking it out is that you grow so much. I am a much wiser person now."

"What did you learn?" I asked.

"Well I wouldn't try to fool anyone by saying it was easy," she said. "I guess I learned how to listen, empathize, and not react. And when I couldn't handle it, I had to remove myself without blaming myself for having done it wrong. I don't know if we would have made it without both of us being really committed and willing to change. I often think I should start a group for the families and friends."

I nodded my head. "Families of trauma survivors desperately need to meet and talk."

She looked me in the eyes. "Anna, you grew up with a father who suffered from PTSD and you know what the family goes through. How about you? You need to write about that."

I thought about what she said for a long time. And that's when I decided to write Part Three of this book. My list isn't complete or in great detail. Many of you no doubt can add to it, but it includes some of my ideas and the ideas of several of my clients, mothers, fathers, wives, husbands, partners, and friends who were in similar situations as you are.

I recommend you read at least Part 1 of this book about post-trauma stress, and also the first two steps in Part 2 of the recovery program, before you read the following suggestions for family and friends. I refer to the family and friends as "you" and to the survivor as "s/he" in most cases.

WHAT YOU CAN DO TO HELP THE PERSON YOU LOVE.

My father lived most of his life with Post-Trauma Stress (PTS). When triggered, he would spend months in what is now known as PTSD, a "disorder." My mother, my sister, and I suffered as well, but my sister and I never knew why until much later. "That's just the way Dad is," we'd say. Years ago it was not acceptable for a man to talk about his emotions and his pain, or show them in any way, or talk about the horrifying events that he had experienced as a refugee. And my mother encouraged my dad's silence. Fearing his terror and intense anger, she would say, "It's no good remembering. It just makes it worse."

Regardless of how hard my father tried to repress his past, I could tell when he remembered. He would scream out in the middle of the night and walk the floor. During the day he became withdrawn, anxious, and depressed. Sometimes he would not speak to us for days. Then he would burst into uncontrollable rages. During those times I was afraid he would commit suicide. When people mentioned some important event in the future, he would say, "I won't live that long." When my sister and I made plans, Dad would become sullen and try to dissuade us. "You never know what's going to happen," he would say. "We might not live that long." He lived to be eighty-eight.

As a child I knew something was wrong, but having no idea what that something was, I thought his problems must be my fault. I watched his every action and reaction and tried to please him and "make him feel better," but regardless of how hard I tried, I was never "good enough" to take away his pain.

Unaware of the pain and the patterns my father had learned as a refugee, I passed too many of them on to my own children. The experience of living with a father who never resolved his PTS damaged my self-esteem, confidence, and zest for life for many years, until I worked with PTSD survivors and discovered how to help myself as well as them. I wanted passionately to help people like my father resolve their issues and live normal happy lives. That way they would not pass on the consequences of their trauma to their children and families. In most cases, together with my clients, we succeeded.

When I asked family members and close friends what they saw as trauma survivor's main issues, invariably they agreed with my friend, Rachel. "Control. They need to feel they have control over their lives."

That's logical, when you think of what many survivors have experienced. They had no control over nature, or an accident, or what others had done to them. Many carry guns everywhere so that they can protect themselves. It is a symbol that states, "I am safe and I am in control of my life."

Untreated PTSD affects the entire family. You are the ones who usually first notice and feel the withdrawal, the

WHAT YOU CAN DO TO HELP THE PERSON YOU LOVE.

isolation, the fear and the anger of your loved one. You are on the receiving end of these feelings. You may be seeing your loved one abuse alcohol and drugs and cause family disruptions. You may be afraid for yourself and your children or see your loved one withdraw into themselves. PTS often causes your loved one to shut down or become numb, and you are left without the person you and the children once knew. And without any support.

Here are some things you can do to help your loved one:

1. If you are a mate or a family member, plan how you can help your loved one reunite emotionally and physically with your immediate family and your extended family after a trauma.

- Lower activity levels initially. When you are together, unplug the phone and focus on each other.
- If you have children, arrange for relatives or friends to keep them for a few days to create some quiet time without stress.
- Cater to your loved one. Cook favorite foods, listen to favorite music, watch favorite TV shows, or do anything you know or learn your loved one enjoys. Ask, don't assume.
- If you are partners, pace yourself with sexual intimacy especially if sexual abuse of some kind was involved in the trauma.

2. Be patient. Decrease your expectations. Remember, recovery takes time. Often a long time. You may think he or she is improving, but then the symptoms get worse again. Forward and backward. Lower your expectations, but don't give up. Usually the relapses occur less frequently over time. If they come less frequently, know that's a hopeful sign.

A person with severe stress after trauma may need to talk about the trauma over and over again. This is part of the recovery process and lessens the charge in the emotional brain (amygdala) over time. (Check Step Eleven on memories in Part 2.) Let your loved one talk, rather than telling him or her to stop going over the past and move on. Refer her or him to a psychotherapist if you have difficulty listening. You might say, "I know you need to talk about this. That's good, but it's really hard for me to listen when I know how much you got hurt. I think it would be really good for you to talk to a therapist. Can you find someone to work with or would you like me to find one for you?" (When someone is severely traumatized she or he may not be able to move forward and act on their own. It's okay for you to take charge at that time.)

3. Give her or him reassurance, love, and compassion. When someone has severe stress after a trauma, s/he is often easily startled and afraid for her or his safety. Reassure the survivor that s/he is safe. Be careful not to surprise your loved one or come up behind the person.

Appreciate who s/he is. What did you love about her or him before the trauma? That person is still there somewhere inside. Survivors very much need loved ones to be on their sides. Tell the survivor that you love her or him and you'll work things out together (but only if that is really what you mean). Read Part One in this book and other books about trauma experiences so you can place yourself into your loved one's "shoes." When you can allow yourself to feel and understand what it would be like to go through similar experiences, then you can become truly compassionate.

4. Be fully aware. It is essential for you to read Part 1 about the nature of PTS and PTSD, so you know exactly what to look for and what to expect. It is much easier to remain calm inside if you know that what is happening is a common part of PTSD and not something specific to him or her. Many people around the world who have experienced severe trauma will react similarly. Also remember that PTS is largely a physical disorder and your loved one is not intentionally trying to hurt you.

If you are concerned that your loved one is withdrawing and has become hopeless and depressed, you are probably afraid s/he might commit suicide. Most often, your loved one does not want to die. S/he wants the pain to stop. Take any talk of suicide seriously, even if it was said in a joking way, especially if s/he carries a gun or has medications that can be used to overdose. Ask him or her questions in a gentle way. If the depression persists, tell your loved one you will make an appointment for the two of you to see the doctor and/or a counselor. If your loved one refuses, there isn't much you can do except see a counselor yourself and ask for advice. The survivor is an adult and can make up her or his own mind. If s/he attempts suicide, call for an ambulance. It is essential to get help, but if something happens, don't blame yourself. Sometimes people show no signs of what they are planning.

5. Ask, don't assume. Ask what your loved one needs from you, what s/he likes, what s/he wants to do, and what is too much. If s/he has nightmares, flashbacks, or outbursts, sit down during a calm time and work out together what you can do and what the children or others can do that would be helpful. Read Part 2, Step One on becoming stable to give you some ideas.

6. Listen and empathize. Although you may believe you have the answers to his or her issues, give no advice unless s/he asks for it. If you hound your loved one, s/he, like anyone else, will get angry and rebel. You can suggest something, but then let it go. If s/he doesn't take your suggestion, know that most of the time s/he isn't quite ready to take that step. It has nothing to do with you personally. So just listen to anything s/he wants to talk about, including what happened during the trauma. And if s/he refuses to talk, encourage the person, but don't push too hard. Let your loved one come out on her or his own, but tell her or him that you are there when or if s/he wants to talk. Place no judgment on what s/he says, unless it is about harming him or herself or someone else. Then you must act.

If you don't feel you can listen to details of the trauma, help him or her seek counseling or a group like a 12 step program or a community or church group where s/he can speak freely and be understood. My mother couldn't handle my dad's refugee experiences, and he learned to be quiet and keep all his feelings inside. He carried the trauma with him all his life. Don't be afraid of your loved one's feelings. Feelings come and go and are normal. So unless s/he becomes violent or hysterical, it's okay for them to be angry or to cry. Most survivors will need to face their emotions sooner or later.

7. Don't take what s/he says or does personally. Not taking your loved one's actions and feelings personally is a big challenge, especially when the person blames you, withdraws, or yells at you. Remember that it may have more to do with his or her symptoms of PTS than anything you have done. Here is a way many people have learned to be able to remove themselves emotionally at that time. Picture yourself standing away from the scene, maybe on a hilltop, watching what is going on. Become a rational, not emotional, adult. Remind yourself that getting emotionally involved will only rush both of you full force into battle or into depression.

When I went into the field of psychology, I learned two ways to defuse anger. They have worked well for me over many years. As a matter of fact, I talked down a Vietnam veteran who was pointing a gun at me once, using these techniques. He had abused his wife several times and blamed me for her finally leaving and going to a shelter.

- Take some of the blame and apologize for what you can honestly see as your part in the problem. Don't give excuses at this point. Come up with a solution. For example, "I can see you are feeling pretty frustrated right now. I'm sorry. You are right that I have not been spending enough time with you. Would it

be okay if we sit down tonight and come up with some ways to change that?" In the evening, sit down and talk about ways both of you can change what is going on. Make sure you carry out your part of the plan.
- Ask several logical and pointed questions about his complaints. Use an adult, non- emotional voice. "Could you tell me exactly what you mean when you say I am not spending enough time with you? How much time do you think we should spend together? What can I do to help make this problem better?"

8. Include your loved one. Don't expect your loved one to resume his or her life as it was before the trauma. Much has happened. Include the person in whatever s/he can handle and is willing or interested in doing. Be realistic, but expect as much functioning as is reasonable.

Have a night once a week you spend together so you can get back in touch with your loved one. If you and your spouse have children and/or limited money, exchange babysitting time with friends. Do things together you both enjoy. When you go out, focus on the things you love about each other. Be honest but not hurtful.

Suggest going out to coffee or to a picnic in the park, take a hike together, go to a football game outside, rent a funny movie, or have dinner with a few friends at your house. Restaurants and places with a lot of people can be very stressful for those with PTS. I'm sure you can think of a lot of other things you can do together.

9. Allow your loved one as much control as you can without hurting you or others. Survivors are often afraid of not being in full control of their lives. That's logical. They are very aware that life is not safe. And if they weren't in control of everything, terrible things could and would happen. Of course, logically you know no one really has control over his or her life. You don't have control over the world, like weather or earthquakes, and lots of accidents. Ultimately you don't have control over other people's feelings, thoughts, and actions. You have control only over your own, and sometimes only tentatively. During recovery, that feeling of the need to control everything in the survivor's life to feel safe again does not automatically go away. It may take a long time.

Back off as much as possible. And how can you do this? By changing your thinking. (Check Part 2, Step Seven.) I counseled a client who had a difficult time allowing his wife who had been in a severe car accident to do some of the things he thought were very controlling of him and the kids. He would get angry, leave, and slam the door behind him. That behavior triggered a cycle of hysteria and then withdrawal in his wife. He wanted to change his reaction. I asked him if there was something he could say to himself each time something happened he felt was controlling.

One day he came in and said that he had finally come to peace with a lot of her controlling behaviors. What he now said to himself over and over again was, "In the light of eternity, how much does this really matter?" Most of the time, he realized that most of her behaviors didn't really matter very much. When they did, he addressed them calmly.

10. Work out your roles again. If you have children, you have no doubt taken on the role of other parent while your loved one was having difficulty functioning. You may have decided to add a second job if your loved one was unable to work, plus be responsible for the home and your children. In many situations, your children may have taken on more adult roles and more responsibilities as well. When your loved one begins to recover, s/he may feel left out and want to return to her or his former position in the family. You and the children may have difficulty shifting these responsibilities back and may feel uncomfortable or even angry at the disruption to your family system. That's normal. The adjustment is often a difficult one and needs to be worked out together in family meetings or in couples' or family therapy with the help of a counselor or chaplain.

11. Deal with trust issues. Do you trust your spouse (or son, or daughter) at this point? You may feel distant from each other, as though you don't know the survivor. You can see s/he has changed, but you don't know what s/he wants and needs at this point. Make sure you are honest (in a kind way) about your feelings and what you think. Then act on your words. You don't trust someone who says one thing and then does another shortly after. Remember, love is freely given, but trust is earned.

A survivor is often jumpy and afraid of touch. A little voice inside tells them touch is dangerous and it startles them. They have great difficulty trusting anyone. Always alert them and make sure they are comfortable with you touching them. If you are partners, you will need to deal with sexual issues. Sometimes a partner doesn't trust that the other person is loyal to him or her. Acknowledge the issue and talk. If your needs and desires have changed, let the person know. But if you can't come to an understanding with each other, seek help.

12. People who are already severely stressed do poorly with increased stress in their lives. Keep stress to a minimum in your lives if possible, but not to the point that it disrupts your life or your family's life. For instance, don't start arguments about things you know will trigger the survivor. If there are problems you know will be very stressful for your loved one, but need to be addressed, it is better to have a third party, such as a minister or counselor, help you deal with the issues together. Be optimistic and think positively. Encourage him or her to go to group meetings or to go out into nature, where s/he can relax.

13. Bring laughter, enjoyment, and humor into your lives. Laughter decreases the stress hormones in your body and changes your outlook on life. Sit down together, if possible, and talk about what you both would like to do to bring laughter into your lives. Watch funny movies or TV shows, especially before bedtime so as not to trigger nightmares. Do activities that you both enjoy and that make you laugh. Take time with friends who like to have fun. Go to the gym together or play tennis. Read funny books or comic books together. Turn work into play and kid around.

Sometimes when someone is depressed, a little distraction helps. Creating something together you both like doing, or encouraging her or him to find a creative outlet such as gardening, art, music, handwork, photography, or anything else you know s/he enjoys, will change her or his hopelessness thoughts and yours, too. (Check Part 2, Step Fourteen and Fifteen, for some ideas.)

14. Ask your loved one what s/he needs from you. Then let your loved one know what you need. At this point in the recovery process it is essential to discover what s/he needs from you. You are only guessing. Yes, you knew each other before the trauma, but both of you have changed. Sit down over a cup of coffee and begin to talk. Ask him or her what you can do to help. Then let him or her know what you need. Keep your requests realistic and simple. If s/he is suffering from severe trauma, your loved one may only be able to help you with your most urgent need, such as giving you a warning that s/he is being triggered. A code word that you agree on, such as "red," will often work for both of you.

15. Look underneath the aggression and drug problems. As I have mentioned earlier, aggression usually comes from a survivor's fear of loss of control in life. Drug use stops the emotional pain and releases a lot of dopamine in the brain so s/he feels better. If your loved one becomes aggressive, either physically or verbally, first of all, try to talk him or her down. But if that doesn't work, leave the situation if you can. Instead of merely looking at the actions, see who your loved one really is, not connecting it to the behaviors. Ask yourself what s/he may be afraid of. In most cases s/he is dealing with the fear of not having control. This triggers feelings of helplessness, and s/he automatically reverts to instinct mode. Some survivors will do almost anything to feel in control again, even to the extent of intimidating and manipulating you. Try to settle your conflicts in a logical and nurturing way. If you can't accomplish this on your own, seek counseling together with your loved one.

If s/he is an addict, encourage her or him to go to counseling, or to Alcoholics Anonymous or Narcotics Anonymous. You may need to attend Al Anon meetings to learn how to deal with your loved one and the situation.

16. Try to anticipate and prepare for your loved one's PTS triggers. Observe him or her and note what you see that triggers the person. Talk about what triggers your loved one and ask what you, the family, and friends can do to help. Common triggers are things that remind the survivor of the trauma. Usually they are people or places, sights, sounds, smells, even the tastes of what the survivor experienced during the trauma. The smell is often the most powerful trigger. Check Part 1 and Part 2, Step One, to learn more about triggers and symptoms of PTS. When the triggers occur, you will know what to expect and you'll be prepared to support your loved one.

17. Set boundaries and enforce them consistently. Sometimes people need motivators to change behaviors especially if they have become addicted to drugs and/or alcohol. It is as important for your loved one as it is for you to set a line that can't be crossed. When both of you are calm, let her or him know quietly what that line is and what will happen if the line is crossed. For instance, you might say, "No physical or emotional violence will be allowed or tolerated with the children or me."

You need to decide what the consequences will be if it recurs, and tell her or him. Then you must carry through with those consequences each time the line is violated. Consistency is essential. You may decide that you and the children will leave immediately for an hour to let your loved one calm down. You might call it a time-out. When you are both calm again, get back together and talk. Work out a word that either of you can say when the other is acting in such a way as to get close to that line. It might be something like "red light" or "stop," or a code word that works for both of you.

If the behavior doesn't change, ask your loved one to come to therapy with you. If s/he refuses, make an appointment for yourself before you decide on a divorce. But if s/he continues to be violent with you or the children, you must take a time of separation until the behavior has changed. If you are the survivor's parent or friend, make sure s/he finds another place to live. You deserve to be safe.

18. Encourage him or her to go for counseling, either alone or with you. There is usually a mental health center close enough for the survivor to attend. Remember, it is often a family member or a loved one who finally gets a survivor to seek help. If you are having relationship issues, ask her or him to come to couples' counseling with you. For therapy to be effective in the long term, *both* of you must want the relationship to improve and *both* must be willing to change.

Without this prerequisite, couples' counseling rarely works. *You* can make changes, but you have no control over your loved ones actions. All you can do is warn the person that you will leave if the behavior doesn't change. However, I don't recommend you threaten to leave unless you are absolutely sure and ready to leave. Make sure you have a plan in place. Seek out individual counseling for yourself before and after if you need to leave.

19. Ultimately you will need to let go. I'm not saying you will have to leave, or that you must stop loving the person. I'm merely reiterating that you can't change another person or that person's behavior. You can only change yourself. The twelve-step programs like AA and Al Anon have a wise saying. "Let go and let God." Lean back and trust something greater than yourself to help you. Another word people often use is *allow*. Allow him or her the opportunity and the right to chose how to live life. If s/he doesn't chose to change or is violent to you and/or the children, I recommend that you separate and get counseling.

WHAT YOU NEED TO DO
TO TAKE CARE OF YOURSELF.

Most of the steps for survivors in Part 2 of this book can help you as well as your loved one, so after you read this list, check them also. Although the twenty steps have been written for survivors, they apply to most people under stress. Select the ones you need and skip those that don't relate to you.

In addition:

1. Balance your life. Many family members say it is exhausting to continuously be available and attentive to their emotionally and/or physically injured loved one. It is exhausting to always be "nice" and to serve someone else. Caretakers have very little time for themselves. Eventually they tend to become depressed, anxious, and ill themselves.

Remember, you are not a robot. You are a human being with feelings, thoughts, and a body that needs restoring. So it is essential to balance taking care of yourself and your loved one. Take an hour or so each day for yourself that has nothing to do with taking care of someone else or with working. The time must be spent on something you want to

WHAT YOU NEED TO DO TO TAKE CARE OF YOURSELF.

do, something that nurtures and renews you, even if it is as simple as reading a book you enjoy or taking a nap. Maybe you like to take a walk in the park by yourself and watch the sunset, or spend some fun time with one of your friends. Maybe you like to exercise, do yoga, play a sport, watch a favorite show or movie, read a book, or do gardening.

One woman I know, who is married to a man who has Alzheimer's, has asked three of her husband's friends to help her. One spends two hours with her husband on Monday, another on Wednesday, and another on Friday. The plan has allowed her to go out for periods of time, take classes, go to the gym, and join a yoga group without worrying about him. She says it has kept her sane.

2. Get involved in projects that excite you and bring out the creative side of you. Read Part 2, Step Fourteen. Being creative often helps stop depression and makes you feel alive. Creativity is actually a need humans have, just like eating and sex. Maybe you like to sing. Join a choir. Or paint. Do woodworking. Take a class. Or act. Join a theater group in your area. Or write. Join a writers' group. Or do photography or filming. Or watch birds. Follow your interests and find new things that excite you. Experiment. Find something that, when you do it, you will lose all sense of time.

3. Reconnect spiritually. Read Part 2, Step Ten. Connecting with God or whatever you call that power in the universe greater than you, can renew your hope and give you peace even in the most difficult times. Do your spiritual practice, meditate, and/or pray each day when you wake up or before you go to bed. It may be a short time or as much as half an hour. Start by thanking God for all the good things you have in life. Your husband, wife, family member or friend is alive and with you today. That's a gift. You live in a democratic country of plenty. Giving thanks is a way of changing your perspective of the day ahead of you.

4. Take time to journal each day. Many of my clients have said that journaling was the most important technique they used to get through difficult times. Often they felt they could not speak to other people about what was going on inside of them, but they could release their feelings and thoughts onto paper. It helped them let go of their worries, anger, fears, and guilt. If you don't want anyone to read your journal, you may wish to take it to work. Keep it somewhere safe. If you prefer you can tear up or burn the pages after you have written them. Burning those thoughts and feelings can actually symbolically help you let them go. Say the words, "I let go of all these thoughts and feelings" as you tear the pages or burn them.

5. Exercise and eat healthy foods. Check Part 2, Step Seventeen. When you are under stress it is often easiest to "veg out" in front of the TV or stop at a fast food restaurant for dinner. But in the long run, doing so daily will create more problems in your life. People who are stressed need more vitamins, especially the B, C, and D vitamins. So take your vitamins daily and eat a healthy diet of green vegetables, fruits, and proteins. Keep your meals simple if you don't want to spend time and energy cooking. Substitute fruit for dessert and snacks.

Create an exercise program that you can do daily, even in front of the TV in the evening if you wish. You may not be fond of doing exercises. If you think of them as boring, it is important to have some distraction in order not to avoid them. Watching TV, listening to a program or music, walking or running outside in a beautiful area, such as a park or the forest, helps.

6. Change your thinking and behavior. Empower yourself and become resilient. Read Part 2, Steps Three, Seven, and Eight. Family members and close friends often begin to think more and more negatively, depending on how their loved ones are doing. You begin to feel like a yoyo and you lose yourself. *S/he's doing well today. I'm doing well today. S/he's doing poorly today. I'm doing poorly today.* Remember, you are not the other person and you are not responsible for her or his problems or actions. You can be willing to help, but you can't make somebody change. You can only be responsible for you, and you can only change your own thoughts and your behavior. The rest you will have to let go.

7. Have an alternate plan. You and your children have a right to be safe and happy. I suggest that any partner who has a potentially violent mate obtain his or her own credit card or have access to enough cash somewhere safe, in case he or she must leave. The same advice is important for friends and for parents who take in their loved one after a severe trauma. If the survivor becomes violent with you or another family member, you may need to have the person move out of your home. Ask for a restraining order, if necessary.

Don't stay with a person who abuses the kids, period. Children are vulnerable and not capable of defending themselves. It is your job as the adult to keep them safe as much as is possible. In order for you to return, s/he must get help first and actually change.

8. Seek counseling if you need help making decisions, or when you need to talk to someone confidentially. A counselor can help you deal with your own issues and can advise you on how to take care of yourself. S/he can also help you work out the lines you must draw in your relationship to feel good about your life. Is it okay for your loved one to drink or do drugs? How much is okay? When do you say no? You may have some friends you can talk to, but make sure you can trust them to keep what you say confidential. Can they listen, be objective, and be realistic and rational instead of merely emotional and trying to control you?

9. If you feel overwhelmed by all you have to do, take time to write a list and prioritize it. Read Part 2, Step Three, on empowering yourself. At the end of the day or the week, you will find that you'll probably not have been able to complete all the items on the list. Make a new list. Instead of worrying about the things you didn't get done, look at all your successes. What did you get done? How might this change your life for the better? Maybe you made an appointment to see a therapist. That's a giant step forward.

10. If possible, attend group meetings with other partners or family members of survivors. The support of a group of people who are experiencing similar issues is very important to your own healing. Usually there are group meetings such as AA or Al Anon, a twelve-step program for codependents, or a church or community group available in your area. If your loved one is a veteran, there will be a VA or Veterans' Center that will have a group meeting for families. The numbers will be in your telephone book or on the Internet. Call them and see what they offer. Go to a couple of meetings before you say it's not for you. But if no group is available in your area, ask around and form a group with similar issues as yours.

You can also look into Internet-based groups and join them. Although meeting face-to-face with other members may be the most ideal way to function as a group, the Internet can be very valuable when you don't have access to a physical group. It may also be that you are a person who would rather speak to a stranger about confidential matters than someone in your own area who might know you or your loved one. Or it may be that, because of your situation at home, you can't leave the house to attend meetings.

11. Don't be afraid of your emotions. Read Part 2, Step Nine, about dealing with emotions. You are human, and part of being human is having emotions. They are normal and are not "bad." They are merely feelings. They are energy in motion and will come and go. It's how you *act* on them that counts. When you are angry, do you lash out at people, or do you go out and mutter to yourself or scream at the sky as you run or exercise to get rid of the energy?

Yes, family members feel anger or deep sadness and fear about what is going on, and that's natural. You may be angry that you must take responsibility for everything, and that others don't understand. You may be grieving for your life the way it was before your loved one's trauma. Or you may be afraid that your loved one will commit suicide.

Underneath anger is often fear. Fear of loss. Fear of the future. How are we going to live? Will s/he ever be able to work again and get a job? Will my loved one always be as emotionally and physically stressed as s/he is now? Will s/he ever stop drinking? Will we ever be close again?

But with the anger and fear is often a feeling of deep grief. A common sadness that families speak of is the grieving for the persons they once knew and who may never return; the grieving of lost expectations; of how they thought their lives would be; and for the hardship they face every day.

If you are feeling any of the emotions I have mentioned, it's not because you are weak. Your problems are real and your feelings are normal. But if you hold all your feelings inside and pretend they don't exist, it is likely that in time they will multiply to such a degree that they will harm you not only emotionally, but also physically. Please get help and do some of the exercises I have listed in Step Nine, so you can release those feelings in a healthy way.

12. Accept yourself, with all your faults and limitations. Check Part 2, Steps Eight and Ten. You're human like the rest of us on this planet. You will make mistakes. In order to

What You Need to Do to Take Care of Yourself.

reduce the stress in your life and feel at peace, you must learn to accept yourself and love yourself. That doesn't mean that you can do anything you wish and continue that negative behavior and still feel good about yourself, but that it is time to forgive yourself for what you have done, honestly apologize, and work on changing your behaviors. Then move on, instead of dwelling on your mistakes and feeling guilty. **You deserve a good life.**

What Your Children Need.

This vitally important section should be a complete book in itself. But because of limited space, I have merely included a few pointers. Look into other resources, too, such as parenting books, child development books, and the Internet for more help, or talk to a counselor who works with children to get advice. Join a group for parents or for families, if available in your community or church. If not, check the Internet for such groups. You will receive both good advice and empathy from people in similar circumstances.

Many children who have a survivor with PTS as a parent experience emotional problems. Depression, anxiety, and acting-out behaviors are common. Your loved one loves the children as much as you do, and s/he does not wish to hurt them in any way, but as with my father, it is inevitable that the children will be affected. Grandparents, if your son or daughter is not willing to talk to the children about what is going on, please take time to do so. No children deserve to grow up thinking that their parents' negative feelings and actions were their fault.

1. **Talk to the children about the survivor's behavior (such as flashbacks and nightmares) and the reasons why s/he is acting the way s/he is.** Explain rationally what is happening.

Young children believe that they are the center of the universe, so if things are not going right, it must be their fault. An adolescent will often feel very angry and may act out or become anxious and depressed. This is not the parent he or she knew. S/he is no fun. Or s/he is mean and controlling and mistreats us. Will my parents get a divorce? Most of the time children are not aware of what is going on inside of them. They have no idea why they are feeling so angry, or why they can't concentrate, or why they are depressed. Typical acting-out behaviors include stealing, skipping school, neglecting homework, getting bad grades, fighting, withdrawing and isolating from family and friends, and doing drugs and alcohol. Check Part 2, Step Two for some other suggestions for dealing with the children.

2. Let your loved one tell the kids what would be helpful to her or him, especially during flashbacks, rages, or times of withdrawal. Talk to your children together. If your spouse is not willing to be part of the discussion, talk to them alone. Talk to all the children, even the young ones, who will pick up the energy around you and the rest of the family.

When my youngest child was not yet of school age, I had a severe attack of arthritis and I'm sure I wasn't always pleasant to be around. My son and his friend often played at our house. They were attempting to be grown-up by getting their own pitcher of juice from the refrigerator. You can guess what happened. Each time they spilled grape juice onto the floor, I would get upset, and they would run and hide. Recently my son and I talked about what had happened. He and his friend had thought they were very bad for spilling things and that they would be punished. I said, "It wasn't because you were being bad that I got angry at you. It was because I had arthritis and I hurt a lot every time I had to bend down and wipe up the juice." I could see the relief in his face as he said, "Why didn't you tell us mom? It would have made a huge difference."

3. Tell them what they can do to avoid triggering the person with PTS. Let them know in simple terms what is happening, what the trauma is about, and why their father or mother has the symptoms s/he has at present. Emphasize that it is not their fault. Then, together with the trauma survivor if possible, talk about how they can help and what they can avoid doing or saying so as not to trigger him or her unnecessarily. Of course, sometimes the children will fail, just as you will fail. You are all humans, so talk about it, reestablish the guidelines, give them a hug, and move on. Overreactions will only make the problem worse.

4. Encourage the children to come to you and ask questions and tell you what is going on. Talk to them, but don't make your spouse the "bad" person. Empathize with them and then take the next step. In many cases, they feel helpless and need a solution. As a parent you are the best person to help them solve the problem. Ask them what they need from you. Sit down and make a list of what the two of you can do to change what is going on. Early in my career I used to counsel many children, adolescents, and families. When I asked the kids what they needed most, the young children might shrug, but the adolescents immediately said. "I need things to change."

See Part 2, Step Three for other problem-solving ideas.

5. Discuss rules and set boundaries for the children, preferably with your mate. Enforce them consistently. You probably set rules and consequences for misbehavior together in the past before the trauma, but now it's time to discuss those limits with him or her and come to an agreement of exactly what they are. Then talk about how the two of you can handle discipline when necessary. Call a family meeting and let the children know clearly what the rules and consequences are.

Make sure your rules and consequences are rational, and that you are willing and able to enforce them. For instance, say you set a rule for an adolescent, and the consequence for breaking it is that the adolescent is grounded and must stay at home after school for the next week. However, both you and your spouse work, so you have no way to make sure that the child is actually at home. In this case, you are asking for trouble. The form of discipline you choose must be one that you can control and enforce. *Be consistent* with implementing the limits you have set. Without consistency, your children learn it's okay for them to break the rules, and that chances are good they'll get away with "bad" behavior.

It is very important that you and your mate support each other in your decisions. If you need to change the rules, try not to criticize each other in front of the children. They must know you are a team and that their parents are in charge. Children need limits and consistency as well as love. It helps them feel secure.

6. Make sure you and your spouse keep your arguments to yourselves. When necessary, take a time-out and find a place by yourselves to talk. Arguments are frightening to children, who are the helpless ones in a family. They are afraid that someone will be violent or will leave and that they have no control over their lives. Often they then bring this anxiety and anger into their schoolwork and relationships, or they withdraw into themselves.

7. Don't hesitate to take your children for counseling. If they don't deal with the issues that are bothering them now, the experience may influence them negatively for a lifetime. Often the most effective way to resolve children's issues is to go to counseling as a family, but I realize that isn't always possible. Either your spouse or one of the children, often an adolescent, will object and refuse to come.

The next most helpful way to resolve children's issues is to see the counselor individually at first, and later together. Children, especially adolescents, need some time of their own with a counselor so they can speak in privacy. The counselor will keep their sessions confidential unless your child wants to tell you what was shared. If possible, have some family sessions together with your children to help resolve your issues at home.

May you and your children flourish and grow in love.

The Healing Wall
(The complete poem)

I.

I ignored the Wall -
for a long time.
I had managed to keep out unwanted reminders
of the memories of what I saw and did and felt
and the Wall threatened to violate this self-truce.
For a while, I refused to go to the Wall.
I came close, but I could not bring myself to go down
into that black hole -
So I stood there alone, on the perimeter
of the large descending block of black, cold stone,
and watched from my vantage point on the hill above.

Concealed by the autumn shadows,
hands pocketed, I turned my back and walked away,
mumbling to myself in a voice so low
even I couldn't hear what I was saying,
"Not today, I cannot do this today."

II.

I visited the Wall.
One evening in the late summer of the year,
when the cool winds blew across the Mall and the
early evening sun was crisp, I went to the Wall, again.
I stood where I had stood before but refused to go,
and without ever deciding,
without ever giving consent
I found myself moving toward it,
pulled by some force I could not see,
drawn by memories I could no longer deny.
I began the slow descent into the dark hole,
not wanting to but needing to go back into
what I had spent twenty-five years trying to forget.

At first tentative, I stood next to the first point of the Wall -
looking down the long descent of widening black granite,
wanting to turn back, but I had committed,
this time I needed to go.
I walked down the path, head down,
unable to look up at the Wall -
afraid I would see a name, recognize a name, any name.
Perhaps a name I had seen before, a death I knew before
his family knew. Perhaps a friend, someone who died and
I didn't know.

I couldn't look but I could feel its presence -
as I descended, it cast a silent, shadow, growing on me.
As the sun went down, the darkness deepened.
I stopped where the walk meets in the middle,

The Healing Wall

joining the two parts of the Wall together -
the deepest part of the Memorial
and slowly, my eyes began their climb up the Wall.
Groove by groove, name by name,
I saw what I knew would be there -
names, hundreds and thousands of names
carved into the cold hard flesh of that stone -
first names and last names
carved by the trauma and devastation of the bombs
and the mines and the sniper fire -
and the yells and the screams
of young men dying and not knowing why.
I heard the haunting sound of the death
of all of those soldiers whose
names I had seen and passed on to those places back
home who would receive the telegram
"We regret to inform you..."
I saw the names, blurred as they were,
I saw them and I could not move.

III.

I touched the wall - down in the deep hole where I stood,
I moved forward - not wanting to
but needing to feel it,
needing to trace the edges of at least one name -
not to remember, but to forget.
I touched the smooth stone, gingerly at first, with one finger
feeling the contrast between that and the rough place where the
stone had been violated by the name carved into it -
and in the stillness of that moment

A Path Beyond Post Traumatic Stress

(I remember the stillness, particularly the stillness),
I did what all who go there must do,
I put my whole hand, palm down, against the stone -
first one hand and then the other, softly first,
Then pressing my palm harder against the Wall until
The full weight of my body leaned against it.
Braced by the stone, held up by its quiet, dignified, strength,
I became connected to the Wall,
connected to everything that happened, everything I had felt,
everything I had avoided for over twenty-five years.
Then I was no longer leaning against the Wall,
I was becoming part of the Wall, or the Wall part of me.
The more I tried to pull away, the more I couldn't move.
It began to pull out of me
emotions I had not felt since I was there,
since that first moment I saw and knew
I had been part of someone's death -
reliving the moment of lost innocence,
remembering the emptiness,
feeling again, the sickness in my heart
I had kept numb for years.
That is when the first tear came, and then a second,
followed by more -
slow tears, warm tears from down deep inside the hole of me.
I became a prisoner of the Wall, captive by its silent,
vigilant, roll call of death.

Then I began to move my hands over the Wall -
over names I did not know,
slow at first, and then faster, almost frantically -
at first not knowing why -

The Healing Wall

but then knowing -
I was looking for one name,
I was looking for the one groove my hands
would know the best,
the one that would confirm what I always knew
to be true but was afraid to admit,
a name that wasn't there but should have been -
mine.

It was that sudden realization,
that revelation of surprise,
when it all rushed in,
when it all came back in on me - overwhelming me,
forcing me to face what I had not been able to face before,
the source of my guilt, my one great sin -
I had lived. I had come back home.
I was no more deserving than any one of these names,
but I had survived.
My hands connected to the Wall,
I gave it back - and the Wall took it, all -
the hurt, the pain, the grief, the guilt, the shame.
For the very first time since coming home -
I cried about the War.

These were not slow tears,
they were fast, they were hot and they burned.
I wept for me and I wept for every single family
and town those names, those grooves, touched.
I leaned against the Wall and it held me up
and I finally let go.

When I was empty, out of tears,
the Wall let go and I pulled away.
I looked around and saw others who had done or
were doing the same as I had done.
Each of us in our own way, letting go.
We looked at each other. We didn't speak, but we knew
and shared, in silence.
It was there, beyond the Wall,
I began to heal.

IV.

I left the Wall
I ascended from that deep hole.
Tired, emotionally exhausted,
I looked back where I had been.
I knew my pain had not magically left me -
I carry it with me today -
but I carry it, it no longer carries me.
This was the healing I could not find before -
The Wall told me my name was not there
and said, "Go live your life, you do not belong here."
And so I do, live my life now, beyond the Wall.

As I turned to walk away,
I overheard a small boy,
unaware of war and all its tragedy,
ask his father - "Why are there so many names
on the wall, Daddy?"
and his father's soft reply echoes in my heart, even now -
because I knew he too knew the Wall

The Healing Wall

the way I knew the Wall -
he replied with the only answer any of us
who have been there have to give -
"I do not know. I do not know."

Epilogue

To this day I do not know why
we have carved so many names on so many walls,
but we have.
What I do know is that there are many casualties of war
we never see carved on walls -
deaths not recorded by grooves chiseled in stone -
kept secret, even from those of us who need to know
the most.
So, as we gather together at this
and all the other walls of war in the world,
let us also honor those of us who lived
with a silent, vigilant, prayer -
a prayer ever present on our lips
and in our hearts...

No more walls, please, no more walls.

© Patrick Overton, PhD, Vietnam veteran
Rebuilding the Front Porch of America

Suggested Readings

Here are a few books that I think might be of particular interest to you. For more suggestions, do an Internet search using terms like books for survivors with PTSD or with post traumatic stress, veterans' experiences, sexual assault, natural disasters, or books to help families. You will find several listed online that could be helpful.

Amen, Daniel G. *Change Your Brain Change Your Life*. Three Rivers Press, New York, New York, 1998
    Scientific evidence that your anger, depression, and anxiety could be connected to how different parts of your brain work.

Cochran, Mark William. *Oby's Wisdom: A Caveman's Simple guide to Holistic Health and Wellness*. Bitterroot Mountain Publishing, Hayden, Idaho, 2012
    From his own experience Dr. M. W. Cochran teaches you how to create the holistic mindset and lifestyle that will lead you to a lifelong state of health.

Landgraf, Laura. *The Fifth Sister: From Victim to Victor - Overcoming Child Abuse*. Empower Press, Oakland, CA, 2015
    Laura's story is as harrowing as it is triumphant as she protects her children from her incestuous father.

Suggested Readings

Maté, Gabor. *When the Body Says No: Understanding the Stress Disease Connection,* John Wiley and Sons, Inc., Hoboken, NJ, 2003
Maté, a medical doctor, reveals and discusses recent scientific evidence that stress effects the body and can create disease. He relates several case studies.

McLay, Robert. *At War with PTSD: Battling Post Traumatic Stress Disorder with Virtual Reality.* Johns Hopkins University Press, Baltimore, MD, 2012
A navy psychiatrist discusses his years of research to create a virtual reality program that can help veterans and military personnel heal from PTSD. He relates the research he has done and his result.

Rothschild, Babette. *8 Keys to Safe Trauma Recovery,* W.W. Norton, New York, NY, 2010
PTSD expert Babette Rothschild lays out eight keys you can use with therapy or on your own to enhance your healing from trauma.

Schwartz, Arielle *The Complex PTSD Workbook* Althea Press, Berkley, CA 2011

Van der Kolk, Bessel *The Body Keeps the Score: Brain, Mind and Body in the Healing of Trauma,* Penguin Books, New York, 2015
This book describes recent scientific advances to show how trauma literally reshapes both body and brain as well as innovative treatments for PTSD.

Zayfert, Claudia and DeViva, Jason C., *When Someone You Love Suffers from Post Traumatic Stress.* Guilford Press, New York, NY. 2011
This is an important book for anyone related to a person who has PTSD.

Acknowledgements

To all the people who have encouraged me, read my drafts, and helped me in the writing of this book, I give a heartfelt thank you. I also thank Jennifer Leo, my editor, and the staff at Bitterroot Mountain Publishing.

I would like to thank all my former teachers, consultants, and especially my clients who have taught me so much about how to cope with the stress that occurs after a severe trauma. I also thank my clients' families who have been willing to open up their hearts to me and have spoken honestly about what has and is happening to them.

I am particularly beholden to Patrick Overton, a Vietnam veteran, educator, and writer who has been willing to share his wisdom and his incredible poem with me to help other survivors of trauma in the recovery process.

Most of all I would like to thank my beloved husband Ronald H. Goodwin, who passed away two years ago. He was my constant support in my many years of working with people who had PTSD, and in my writing. I miss him every day.

About the Author

E. Anna Goodwin M.S, NCC is a former psychotherapist, lecturer, workshop presenter, and writer. In her private practice she specialized in working with clients who came in with symptoms of severe stress after a trauma. Her clients included children, adults, couples, and families who had experienced different traumas such as war, abuse, accidents, and natural disasters. She has taught at two universities, lectured, and conducted a variety of workshops in several states using her extensive knowledge of PTSD.

CPSIA information can be obtained
at www.ICGtesting.com
Printed in the USA
JSHW011217010819
1012JS00004BA/7